DEALING WITH CRIME AND AGGRESSION AT WORK

DEALING WITH CRIME AND AGGRESSION AT WORK

A handbook for organizational action

written by
Peter Reynolds

McGRAW-HILL BOOK COMPANY

London · New York · St Louis · San Francisco · Auckland
Bogotá · Caracas · Lisbon · Madrid · Mexico · Milan
Montreal · New Delhi · Panama · Paris · San Juan
São Paulo · Singapore · Sydney · Tokyo · Toronto

Published by
McGRAW-HILL Book Company Europe
Shoppenhangers Road, Maidenhead, Berkshire, SL6 2QL, England
Telephone 0628 23432 Fax 0628 770224

British Library Cataloguing in Publication Data
Reynolds, Peter
  Dealing with Crime and Aggression at
  Work: Handbook for Organizational Action
  I. Title
  364

  ISBN 0-07-707932-9

Library of Congress Cataloging-in-Publication Data
The cataloging-in-publication data of this title is available
from the Library of Congress, Washington DC, USA

12345 BL 97654

Typeset by BookEns Ltd, Baldock, Herts
and printed and bound in Great Britain by Biddles Ltd, Guildford, Surrey.

Contents

Foreword

According to Home Office research one in five of us becomes a victim of crime each year. Wherever the crime happens, the effect can be devastating. Not only do we have to endure physical pain, financial loss or emotional suffering, we also have to come to terms with the fact that this has been caused by the conscious act of another human being. Victims often feel angry, guilty or frightened. They may blame themselves for what has happened or put the blame on those in authority who, they believe, could have prevented it.

Although the effects of crime are more serious than is usually recognized, this book shows that the help which victims need is often straightforward. Many victims do not need qualified counsellors or therapists in order to recover from the experience and resume their normal lives. Once the impact of crime and the needs of victims have been understood, most employers will be able to develop very effective strategies to support their own staff following a crime.

Crime in the workplace has been a major issue of concern for Victim Support for several years. The early Victim Support schemes dealt largely with people referred by the police after an incident at home or in the street. There was an assumption that incidents in the workplace were rare, and that they were adequately dealt with by the employer. However, as Victim Support became increasingly well-known both employers and staff started approaching us for help after an incident. A number of important factors started to emerge.

Firstly, we found that workplace crime was more widespread than anyone had believed. We were approached by victims of serious assaults and incidents such as armed raids, but also by people who had been subject to intimidation, threats and verbal abuse, sometimes on a daily basis. Victims contacted us not only from the retail sector and from banks and building societies, but from a wide range of small businesses and statutory organizations.

Secondly, we found that victims of crime in the workplace face particular problems. Following a crime it is human nature to try and find an explanation for what has happened, and to protect against it happening again. People who have been burgled frequently respond by improving the security of their homes. People who have been attacked in the street will often change their route to avoid the area where the incident happened. However, people who become victims of crime in their workplace often have no control over where they work, or how they are protected at work. They have to go back to the scene of the crime day after day.

Lastly, we found that many victims felt that they had been insensitively treated by their employers. They complained that they felt blamed for what had happened, or that their distress was simply ignored.

We were also approached by a number of employers, anxious to improve the treatment of their staff following a crime. They had often given considerable thought to crime prevention strategies, but realized that even if nothing was stolen or damaged, the crime still had an impact on their staff.

In 1990 Victim Support organized a national conference on the theme of violence in the workplace, attended by representatives from a wide range of commercial and statutory organizations. The key-note speech was given by the then Home Secretary, David Waddington, who highlighted the cost of workplace crime and the importance of care for victims. He urged employers to take urgent action.

Following the conference Victim Support started working with both statutory and commercial organizations in response to requests for advice, consultancy and training.

Last year, through our trading company Victim Support Limited, we launched a training initiative for employers concerned about victims of workplace crime. Peter Reynolds is one of several consultants who work in co-operation with Victim Support staff to run tailor-made training packages for business and public sector organizations.

Of course, many organizations cannot afford training or in-house counselling for employees, and do not have the staff to organize complex post-incident procedures. There is still plenty which even the smallest organizations can do to ensure that victims are treated with sensitivity and understanding.

This book will help people in small and large organizations to understand the impact of crime and to think about ways in which the employer can respond. This is the first book of its kind, and I believe it is essential reading for anyone who is concerned about crime in their workplace.

Helen Reeves OBE
Director
Victim Support

Preface

My first professional contact with victims of violence and crime at work happened in the autumn of 1986. I still remember the first case vividly. At our initial meeting, unable to make the journey to my office alone, he was accompanied by his wife. It was clear that their lives had been broken by an extremely violent incident at work. Furthermore, over the months that followed it seemed as if everything else conspired to victimize him time and time again.

During those same months other cases also started to present—at first in odd ones and twos, but slowly growing to become a significant part of my caseload. These were significant not just numerically but also because of the depth of their distress. Admittedly my role at that time as a counsellor meant I would be likely to come into contact with such victims more than most other people within an organization; however, I became concerned at the increasing numbers of such cases. By the late 1980s I realized that this was not an isolated phenomenon and must be merely the tip of a much greater problem, yet obtaining accurate figures to assess the size of the problem was (and still is) extremely difficult.

Equally at that time, literature relevant to violence and crime at work was very thin, amounting mainly to specialist articles and academic papers on post-traumatic stress disorder. Studies on violence and crime at work were few and far between. Furthermore, the related issue of what organizations can do in response was untouched.

Since then the picture has changed somewhat, considerable work has been carried out with individual victims and the literature relating to supporting and helping victims is much richer. However, the related issue concerning organizational strategies remains barren. This book is an attempt to start to fill the gap. The primary focus here concerns practical policies and strategies which organizations can adopt to tackle violence, crime, aggression and abuse of staff at work. It is not a text about the techniques and methods of therapy and support. These are topics that are adequately covered elsewhere by other authors.

However, without wishing to demean in any way the role of professional therapists, in many cases such specialist skills are not required. With appropriate training and guidance much can be offered by ordinary people. In an organizational setting this usually means managers, supervisors, other specialist staff (e.g. security and personnel) and colleagues. Indeed, providing this type of training has become an important aspect of my current work as an independent consultant. However, I am also aware that if this type of lay help is to prove effective, it needs to be coordinated within a sensible framework.

Although the detail of this framework will vary from one organization to another, there is, I believe, an underlying sequence of steps that can be used to steer any action. Describing this sequence will be an important task in the pages that follow. Each chapter will outline step by step both the essential background information and the actions that need to be considered as a result, eventually culminating with an overall strategy for organizational action.

Perhaps it is also worth mentioning at this point my association with Victim Support. As an organization, Victim Support is very widely known as the national body which provides help for victims (and their families) who have been affected by crime in general. Perhaps less well known is the Victim Support 'Crime at Work' initiative. This was started in 1993 as a direct result of approaches made by organizations seeking help for staff who had become victims of violence and crime at work. As a result a small team (consisting of full-time Victim Support staff and specialist consultant trainers) was set up to offer organizational help. As a member of this team it made sense when writing this text to seek formal endorsement by Victim Support for the approach outlined here. Obviously I am delighted with their support.

Hopefully the text will appeal to a wide audience. This is likely to include a number of specific groups; firstly, general managers, personnel and security or other specialist staff who become directly involved with victims following an incident; secondly, senior managers and personnel or Human Resource Development (HRD) managers who are responsible for designing policies and procedures in the event of workplace incidents; thirdly, training staff who become involved in designing and delivering training on security or incident procedures; and finally other specialists such as counsellors who are actively working in the field. Furthermore, I have attempted to address a wide range of different work settings. As such I hope the text will appeal to commercial, public and voluntary sectors—hopefully, any work environment where staff are at risk.

Finally, I would like to close this preface with a plea for action. Despite the efforts of both the police and government, in general violence and crime are increasing both at work and elsewhere. I believe it has now reached a point where the effects can no longer be ignored. While organizations like Victim Support offer invaluable help for victims of crime in general, the responsibility for supporting victims of violence and crime at work must remain with the employer. As I hope to demonstrate, the investment needed to provide effective help need not be enormous. For the organizations, taking action makes sense commercially by minimizing any avoidable costs that result from violence and crime. For the individual victim, taking action makes sense by speeding up their recovery. However, action is needed now. Victims who suffer unnecessarily because of an incident at work seem to me to pay a very high price for (what should have been) a normal day at work. Being ignored afterwards compounds their plight still further.

If the text that follows stimulates every reader to do something to make sure that violence and crime is put on the agenda where they work, then my efforts at writing will have been amply rewarded.

Acknowledgements

I suspect that very few books are written by authors who are isolated from the ideas and influence of others. This text is no exception. Although many people have helped both directly and indirectly along the way, some deserve a special mention. Firstly, there are all of the people who gave their time and energy which enabled me to write the specific organizational case studies in Chapters 11 to 13. Without their help in providing real life examples this text would have been merely an exposition of my thoughts on 'what could be'. They include:

From the 'Leeds'	— David Richards
	— David Jarrett
	— Adrian Drysdale
From Argos	— Graham Ledward
	— Ian Harley
From Redsands Children's Centre	— Roy Grimwood
	— Sue Clifton

Next I must include Victim Support, whose director Helen Reeves has provided a foreword to the book. Jane Cooper, Mark Robertson and Anne Viney have provided detailed critique, comments and suggestions.

I must also mention two close friends and colleagues who often act as my own personal and professional support, Bill Evans and Jane Sonntag. Without their support and tolerance this text would never have reached completion. Equally my immediate family, Barbara, Jennifer and James, cannot be ignored. They, more than most, have lived with my morose behaviour during the periods when the words refused to flow. The publishers, McGraw-Hill, also deserve a mention—in particular, Julia Riddlesdell for giving me the forum to allow this topic to reach a much wider audience.

Before closing, I have to include a few special words for Penny Grimshaw. I came to know Penny during her employment as the first Counselling Coordinator at the 'Leeds'. I know her understanding, compassion and gentle way of working with people was valued beyond words. For me Penny became a mentor and a source of inspiration, ideas and insight. I owe her a very deep debt of thanks.

Finally and perhaps most important of all, I must mention the many victims who have permitted me to gain an insight into their personal private suffering. It would be wrong of me to mention any by name; however, they more than anyone have helped mould and extend my thinking. I know in many cases their struggle has been both heroic and unrecognized. I only hope that the ideas presented here will help to minimize the struggle for others who suffer in the future.

Peter Reynolds

Introduction

A PROBLEM WORTH ADDRESSING?

Consider the fact that in 1992-3 the British Retail Consortium reported that in the retail sector alone:[1]

- A total of 14 000 staff were subjected to physical violence and a further 106 000 to threats of violence.
- In total, there were 2.1 million criminal incidents—1.5 million involving thefts by customers.
- The total cost of retail crime was around £2 billion.

Is violence and crime a problem worth addressing? With figures like these, the answer has to be 'yes'. Workplace crime is a major issue; furthermore it occurs in all shapes, types and sizes. It ranges from relatively minor incidents involving loss of property through to loss of life; it also involves many types of companies from those who are everyday household names through to the shops on the local parade. Indeed, while I was working on the outline for this text, a news bulletin one evening reported that a Group 4 security guard delivering wages to a company had been murdered during an armed raid. This is an issue that can no longer be ignored. In my view it is tragic that criminal incidents are now so commonplace that unless they are exceptional, unusual or particularly brutal they no longer make even the front page of regional newspapers, let alone the headlines. Criminal incidents victimize both the organization and the individuals involved; both can pay a very high price.

The intention of this book is to help organizations look at the problem and respond effectively. I will argue later that it is a problem that affects an increasing number of organizations and employees every year. However, most readers will probably never have been directly involved in an incident themselves. If this is the case and you have no first-hand experience of how crime can affect victims they try to complete the following exercise before reading any further.

Exercise 1.1
Sit back for a few moments, close your eyes and try to recollect a vivid memory which has stuck in your mind—for example, a car accident; if you have children, the birth of your first child; hearing the news about the death of someone close to you; perhaps even (for those who are old enough) what you were doing on the day that President Kennedy was assassinated.

Whatever the event you have chosen no doubt you can remember it in vivid detail—what kind of day it was, where you were, what you were doing, who else was with you, what was said, perhaps even what you were wearing. Indeed, if the memory is particularly strong you might even find yourself experiencing some of the emotions and feelings you experienced at the time.

Although there is some debate about the mechanism of vivid memories, there is no question that they exist. Yet they are mild by comparison with being involved in (or at the scene of) a criminal incident. Discovering that your lorry full of electrical goods has disappeared or being confronted by someone using threatening language (and often using abusive swear words), perhaps wielding a baseball bat, knife, machete, firearm or plastic carrier bag which they say is full of explosive, creates a very vivid memory. Furthermore, it will be a memory that is vastly greater in magnitude than any of the examples in the previous exercise. Such memories can also be intrusive and debilitating, in some cases severely damaging both the individual involved (either directly or as a witness), their relationships with others, both at home and at work, and their capacity to function normally as a human being. In short the human costs for victims of crime can be devastating.

However, this is not the end of the story. Where incidents happen at work then the organization suffers as well. It will experience:

- Disruption of daily operations
- Direct costs of any loss of goods or money where an incident involves robbery
- Costs of repair or replacement of property or equipment where damage occurs during the course of an incident
- Consequent inflation of future insurance premiums
- Sickness absence costs if staff are off work following the incident
- Costs of employing relief staff to cover any absence (perhaps involving premium rates of pay)
- Lowered morale of staff (particularly if they are repeatedly exposed to incidents)
- Perhaps higher levels of staff turnover and/or requests for transfer to other duties
- Difficulties in recruiting new staff as word gets round about the risks involved for staff employed by the company
- High stress levels for staff involved in high-risk jobs

All of these costs, both human and organizational, make even a single incident a matter for serious concern. Yet sadly nowadays we are no longer talking about isolated incidents. Chapter 2 will highlight that the numbers of incidents which occur are increasing annually. Indeed, they have now reached such a proportion that for many organizations they pose a very real problem. Furthermore, the range of organizations and professions affected now extends to practically every corner of commercial and industrial life. Few (if any) can claim immunity, even organizations which were once comparatively safe are now under threat (e.g. estate agencies, schools and even professional sports men and women are sometimes attacked by rivals and/or spectators, etc.).

This is the substance of this book. Chapter 2 looks at the frequency of violence and crime at work together with the types of organizations that are affected (and the types of employees who are affected). With this as a backcloth, Chapter 3 examines the effects of violence and crime on an organization. Chapter 4 follows by looking at how organizations can monitor incidents. Chapter 5 addresses how to minimize incidents together with measures to manage aggression and abuse more effectively. Once the first five chapters have examined in detail the organizational aspects of violence and crime, Chapter 6 will discuss the effects on victims and witnesses. Chapters 7 and 8 provide guidelines on practical organizational responses to incidents, including providing an immediate post-incident response procedure and longer term follow-up and support. Additionally, the dilemma faced by small businesses will be highlighted. Their situation is very different to that of the large organization and of very real concern as often they do not have the resources to address crime and violence in any concerted way.

Hopefully, by this stage it will also have become evident that whatever approach is adopted, there are considerable training implications. These will be the theme for Chapter 9. Finally, Chapter 10 will attempt to pull together all of the various strands within the book into a cohesive framework for how an organization can start to address violence and crime at work. Last of all, to bring this alive, Chapters 11 to 13 will outline three extended organizational case studies which illustrate current examples of how different organizations have started to tackle the issue.

As far as possible, the text will be illustrated with organizational examples, exercises and anonymous case studies. Also, as this is an area which is plagued by unhelpful, but commonly held, myths, these will be highlighted at appropriate points within the text.

Crime in the workplace has tended to be cloaked in a veil of secrecy. However, I believe it is a topic that deserves open discussion and a much higher profile. Most managers are intensely concerned when one of their staff is involved in an incident. Unfortunately they are often at a loss as to how to respond. Above all they fear they may do something which will make matters worse. As a result they frequently do nothing. However, 'doing nothing' is often interpreted by victims as 'not giving a damn'. It also increases their sense of isolation and despair.

To draw this introduction to a close and at the same time illustrate some of the points made earlier I will relate the case of just one employee who suffered through crime at work. Although the case is very serious and quite lengthy it introduces many points which will be examined more closely later. Also, as with all of the case studies concerning individuals, names have been changed and some of the details modified to protect the anonymity of those actually involved. Furthermore, as some of the case studies are quite harrowing, I have tried to avoid burdening the reader with too much 'blood and guts'. If, as a consequence, the reporting style seems too clinical it is because I do not wish to be accused of unnecessary sensationalism. Nevertheless, as you read through the case which follows try to think about what you would have done had this man been one of your employees or colleagues.

Case Study 1.1

John was one of two men involved in a cash delivery service to local branch offices. Early one afternoon they were asked to deliver a substantial sum of money to an office in a local suburb. As the road at the front of the office was busy they turned into a car park at the rear. John remained in the van while his colleague went to the back door of the office. On reaching the door he signalled 'all clear' and John left the van carrying a case of money. Within seconds four assailants struck, two attacking each man with pickaxe handles/baseball bats. John let go of the bag, activated his personal alarm and tried to protect himself as best he could. Despite this he was clubbed to the ground, sustaining very severe bruising to his forearms, shoulders and upper body together with a laceration to his scalp requiring some 14 stitches. He was detained in hospital overnight for observation but allowed home the following day.

Sadly this was only the prelude; over the next three years much more was to follow. John's physical wounds healed relatively quickly; his memories and psychological scars did not. Although the police investigation was thorough they were sensitive and understanding of John's condition. Throughout the first few months he was plagued with intrusive, flashback memories. On an evening, if he went to his local pub he could only remain with people for around half an hour and even then he had to find a spot where he could have his back against a solid wall. If someone out running passed him while he was walking home he experienced extreme anxiety—imagining the attack was about to happen all over again. Every time he turned on the television or picked up a newspaper it seemed to be reporting a similar incident to his own. Needless to say, it rekindled memories of the incident as if it had only happened yesterday. At night John fell asleep easily but was awake again within an hour or two. Finally he resorted to watching 'safe', non-violent videos in the middle of the night until exhaustion set in. Despite his GP's best efforts even medication was no help. As one might expect after many weeks of this disturbed behaviour John's relationship with his family began to deteriorate as well.

The author became involved with John's case some seven months after the incident. Although at that time he was still severely traumatized, over the next two or three months he did make substantial progress. John eventually returned to work some 10 months after the attack. At first he found it difficult but as the weeks elapsed it became easier. Unfortunately, however, after about 6 weeks a new supervisor asked him to carry out a similar duty to the one where the incident occurred. John collapsed and was sent home. The following day he saw his GP and was 'signed off' as sick—he never returned.

A few weeks into the second period of absence John was required to attend a DSS medical review to assess his case and degree of disability. When asked to recount what happened he panicked and became incoherent. As a result the author suspects that only a fraction of his story was verbalized. His physical wounds had long since healed and he was assessed as 10 per cent disabled as a result of the experience. An appeal was lodged. The GP and the author provided evidence and eventually after two further medical reviews (involving similar anxiety for John) his case was reassessed at 60 per cent disability. However, this whole procedure took a further 12 months. In the meantime other events were to unfold.

Throughout this period John's condition was little better than shortly after the incident. He was referred for psychiatric help, but even this was little help. It seemed that with every step forward some other event happened which caused one setback after another.

During the summer of that year John went abroad on holiday. Even making the decision to go filled him with anxiety—he was afraid the DSS would withhold benefit if they found out. Both his GP and the author pledged this would not be the case. When he returned his house had been burgled.

Some 18 months after the incident John was finally retired on grounds of ill health. It was clear he would never be able to return to his original job. Everyone involved hoped this would mark a new beginning, but yet again other events frustrated any progress. For example, following retirement, when John's car insurance was due for renewal the insurance company withheld cover because he had retired prematurely as a result of an extreme anxiety state. Once again this prompted further intervention by the GP and the author.

The GP and author's greatest fears followed the arrest of two men some two years after the incident. When John was asked to take part in an identity parade his anxiety became extreme. Thankfully he was never summoned to give evidence in court. I am sure that it would have proved to be the final straw.

Over the months that followed John did start to make some progress. The memories slowly became blurred and less vivid and he began to rebuild his life. However, he will never be the same again. The experience has scarred and disabled him for life. Even today the story is not complete as Criminal Injuries Compensation still remains to be settled. Unlike many of the stories on television this case does not have a happy ending; in the meantime John soldiers on.

Thankfully most cases are not as extreme or complicated as this, but in their own way most criminal incidents involve some level of distress for those involved. Furthermore, many features and complications in John's case recur time and time again. The chapters that follow will highlight these in greater detail together with providing practical guidelines for how to deliver effective help. However, perhaps the first sensible step is to look at the problem from an organizational viewpoint to establish the size and extent of the problem. This will be the topic for Chapter 2.

SUMMARY

- Crime at work is a significant problem. It affects both the staff involved and the organization—both are victimized as a result.
- Being involved in a criminal incident (either directly or as a witness) creates extremely vivid memories. These can be both intrusive and debilitating and in some instances the consequences can be devastating.
- Where criminal incidents happen at work, then the organization will also pay a high price.

- Most managers are intensely concerned when one of their staff is involved in an incident. However, they often do not know how to respond.

2

The extent of violence and crime

TYPES OF VIOLENCE AND CRIME AT WORK

Before starting to look at the extent of crime at work we really ought to be sure we know what we are talking about. The term 'criminal incident' is often used loosely as if there is common agreement on what it means. However, defining crime at work precisely is not as easy as it first appears. To illustrate this difficulty try to complete the following exercise before reading any further.

Exercise 2.1
Spend a few minutes thinking about and writing down what you would define as a criminal incident at work. Next make a list of as many different types of criminal incidents as you can think of which could happen in a work context.
   When you feel your list is complete, re-examine it in the context of your original definition. Does the definition cover all of the incidents on your list or do some stand out as anomalies?

Defining and categorizing 'crime' is notoriously difficult. When re-examining your list of incidents in the previous exercise you might have found yourself rewording your original definition. Defining crime comprehensively is not easy. Different people have different definitions; what is a crime to one person (or in one organization) may be borderline to another. Equally different people and/or different organizations will be sensitive to different types of incidents.

The catalogue of crime at work covers a huge range of different types of incidents, including:

- Crimes against property, e.g.
  - where industrial or commercial premises are burgled and goods, information or money is stolen
  - hijacking and theft of vehicles and/or their contents (often HGVs carrying valuable goods)
  - shoplifting, sometimes petty but nowadays increasingly systematic and ruthless: e.g. shoplifting to order
  - theft at work where personal belongings are stolen (e.g. wallets, handbags, credit cards, clothing, etc.)
  - vandalism and arson where property or equipment is deliberately/maliciously damaged or destroyed
- Crimes against the person, e.g.:
  - incidents involving robbery, armed assault or malicious assault
  - less serious assaults (which might not even be reported)
  - incidents involving manslaughter and murder
  - sexual assaults
  - kidnapping or hostage-taking of either employees or their families
- Crimes by an employee(s), e.g.:
  - theft from other employees or the organization
  - acting in collusion with other villains who commit any of the crimes previously mentioned (either by passing on vital information or by direct involvement themselves)
  - withholding information about internal crimes, e.g. as in the recent inquiries into systematic child abuse in children's homes
- Computer crime and fraud, e.g.:
  - where accounts or financial systems are systematically falsified, usually for monetary gain
  - where computer programs are deliberately corrupted either with malicious intent or the intention of stealing either information or money

- Crimes which have a terrorist intent, e.g. where an employee is forced to carry a bomb or explosive device to a designated place or to relay information to some authority at a pre-designated time
- One could also argue that other crime which takes place outside of the workplace often has an impact back at work—perhaps through employees needing time off—or simply being unable to concentrate when at work.

The catalogue is enormous. However, it would be wrong to conclude that all of these types of events are major issues in all organizations. They are not. Indeed, in some ways it is ironic that the more horrific and exceptional cases receive the most press and media coverage, yet such cases are not typical. Having said this I would hasten to add that in no way do I wish to minimize the experience of anyone involved in an exceptional event. Their lives can be ruined as a result. However, they are comparatively rare. Murder, manslaughter and kidnapping does happen, but thankfully it is still comparatively rare. The vast majority of incidents go unreported or at best are reduced to a few column inches somewhere on the inside pages of local newspapers.

Instead of focusing on types of criminal incident (which actually requires considerable knowledge of criminal legislation), some authorities focus on the distinction between violent and non-violent incidents. However, defining what is violence at work is equally as problematic as defining crime at work. To illustrate this, three definitions are included below:

1. 'Purposeful or reactive behaviour intended to produce damaging or hurtful effects physically or emotionally, in other persons.' (*Violence to Staff Handbook*, Family Services Units, 1989)[2]
2. 'The application of force, severe threat or serious abuse, by members of the public towards people arising out of the course of their work whether or not they are on duty.'
   It includes:
   'Severe verbal abuse or threat where this is judged likely to turn

into actual violence; serious or persistent harassment (including racial or sexual harassment); threat with a weapon; major or minor injuries; fatalities.'
('Violence to staff', Report to the DHSS Advisory Committee, 1988)[3]

3. 'Any incident in which an employee is abused, threatened or assaulted by a member of the public in circumstances arising out of the course of his or her employment.'
('Violence to staff', HSE Pamphlet, 1988)[4]

These definitions are useful in that they broaden the scope of incidents to include events such as verbal abuse from customers (or managers for that matter), being spat at, etc. None of these events can be classified as crimes but, as will be pointed out later, they are far more common than actual physical threat or injury.

It is also interesting to note that the second two of these definitions confine violence to incidents arising from members of the public. Therefore, one presumes, they would not include bullying, systematic (or casual) harassment or abuse by colleagues, subordinates or managers, etc. They assume that violence is perpetrated by an external source. However, even more important is the danger inherent in this kind of approach; it can easily lead to the assumption that violent incidents are more important than non-violent or, that victims of violence will be more affected than victims who are not subjected to violence. Furthermore, assumptions can quickly become widely accepted myths, e.g.:

'Crimes (or violence) directed against persons are more damaging than crimes (or violence) against property.'

This is both misleading and quite simply wrong! Admittedly, sometimes violence leads to horrendous consequences for victims with their lives being devastated as a result, but sometimes it does not. For example, the author recalls a recent conversation with a colleague where the colleague casually mentioned that he had been mugged four times. Although it may be difficult to believe, he

---

simply put it down as a fact of life for anyone who chose to drink in city centre pubs.

Crimes or violence against property can also lead to an equally wide range of reactions. Some people are largely unaffected whereas others may be devastated. For anyone who doubts the impact of non-violent crime at work I would suggest they try talking to either one of the Maxwell pensioners or a business owner who has experienced serious corruption or loss of information stored on computer files by a vindictive programmer who introduced a 'virus' into the system. Businesses have failed as a result.

In a similar vein some organizations make a distinction in the degree of violence involved in an incident. They distinguish between 'clean' incidents (which generally involve threat alone) and 'dirty' or 'nasty' incidents (which usually involve physical contact with an assailant or assault). Yet again this can lead to a similar myth that 'clean' incidents have less impact on people than 'dirty' ones. Once again this is both misleading and wrong. Some people are severely affected by 'clean' incidents and some are not, and similarly with 'dirty' incidents. Furthermore, while on this point, it is worth highlighting the fact that although jargon like 'clean' and 'dirty' can be a useful form of shorthand for describing incidents, it must be used with care when talking to victims. People may well perceive it as an insult to their experience.

Given the difficulties that arise when defining and classifying crime and violence, I must return to the original question, 'What does crime at work involve?' Adopting a broad brush approach, I would respond by saying that usually there is little disagreement over what constitutes major crime or significant violence at work. For example, hijacking and armed assault are invariably perceived as crimes. The difficulties arise at the fringes—'is it one type of incident or another?' or with 'low key' issues such as 'when does vociferous disagreement become a threat?' and 'when could a verbal threat be categorized as violent?' Yet beyond these academic distinctions there is a more fundamental issue to be taken into account; i.e. the choice of definition will influence the types of event that are taken into account and recorded.

This is an important consideration when setting up a monitoring system for incidents at work which we will return to later in the section 'how to start'. For the present there are other questions like 'how big is the problem?' and 'what kind of organizations are affected?' that need to be addressed first.

TYPES OF ORGANIZATIONS AFFECTED

The number and types of different organizations affected by crime at work is huge. Practically every organizational sector is affected to some degree. By glancing at the catalogue of criminal incidents listed earlier a brief indication of the range of organizations at risk is given (see Table 2.1). Simply considering this group of crimes alone, it is clear that as far as crimes against property are concerned, no organization is immune.

Table 2.1   The range of organizations at risk

Type of incident	Organizations at risk
Burglary	All organizations—large and small, from multi-national giants working in large industrial and office complexes to sole traders working from home
Hijacking/theft of vehicles	Any organization which owns, leases or hires vehicles, delivers their own goods or delivers goods on behalf of others (e.g. haulage companies)
Shoplifting	Any shop—from the 'out of town' hypermarket to the local newsagent and tobacconist at the street corner
Theft at work	See examples given for burglary above
Vandalism and arson	See examples given for burglary above

Simply considering this group of crimes alone, it is clear that as far as crimes against property are concerned, no organization is immune.

Perhaps, rather than identifying an enormous list of organizations affected by crime and violence, it would be more useful to look at which occupations are at risk. In this respect the Health and Safety Executive[5] give a useful checklist (see Table 2.2)

Table 2.2 Occupations at risk

Type of activity	Occupational type
Handling money or valuables	Cashiers
	Delivery staff
	Transport workers
	Bank and Post Office staff
	Commissionaires
	Security staff
	Shop assistants
Providing care, advice or training	Nurses
	Ambulance staff
	Social workers
	Teachers
	Housing Office staff
Carrying out inspection or enforcement duties	Traffic wardens
	Ticket inspectors
	Park keepers
Working with mentally disturbed, drunk or potentially violent people	Prison officers
	Landlords
	Mental health workers
Working alone	Home visitors
	Taxi drivers
	Domestic repair workers

A glance through any popular newspaper on any working day will usually confirm that one or more of these occupational groups has been subjected to a criminal/violent incident at work. For example, this particular section was written on Thursday 24 June 1993; ignoring other domestic incidents, the *Yorkshire Evening Post*[6] on the same day reported:

- 'Building Society Shooting Terror'—Building Society employees were threatened by two masked raiders with guns. The report gives a graphic account of how one of the staff had a gun put to his head and was threatened with being shot but instead the raider 'blasted out a video screen'.
- 'Traffic Warden in Strike Threat'—a pay dispute based on 'wardens coming under increasing physical attacks but being consistently refused new pay grades'.
- 'Jail for Man in Gun Drama'—a report of a trial where the accused 'waved a replica revolver at police officers', though no doubt at the time of the incident the officers involved did not recognize that it was a replica.
- Burglars broke into a school and stole a video and cash.
- Burglars forced an entry into a home-based office and stole £8000 worth of equipment.

No doubt a similar pattern can be found in every other popular newspaper throughout the country. For anyone who still has lingering doubts or believes the case is being overstated then I suggest they carry out a similar exercise with any local paper (perhaps over two or three weeks to obtain a more representative sample of incidents) and look at the outcome for themselves.

To return to the original question, 'What kind of organizations are affected?', I suggest that *all* organizations are at risk from crimes against property and crimes committed (or aided and abetted) by employees. Furthermore, companies that employ anyone in the types of occupational roles highlighted earlier will also bear an additional risk. The section that follows will try to assess the magnitude of this risk.

However, before moving on there is one further point which is worth mentioning at this stage. This concerns the issue of staff protection, i.e. whether staff in high-risk jobs should be given additional protection. The following myth is widely believed.

> *'Well-protected people, premises or security vehicles minimize the likelihood of an incident taking place.'*
>
> Wrong again—there is no simple correlation between provision of protection and the incidence of crime or violence. Protection may provide a greater sense of security for staff (and for that reason alone may be worth carrying out), but it does not take away the risk of an incident occurring. Furthermore, although there is no proof of this, some security experts are convinced that the greater the degree of protection provided for staff, then the greater the degree of force/violence which villains are likely to employ during an incident. In security jargon, 'the harder the target the harder it could be hit'.
>
> *With crime and violence at work there are **no** simple solutions.*

THE SIZE OF THE PROBLEM

The illustration from the *Yorkshire Evening Post* in the previous section suggests that the problem is big. If five serious incidents are reported in a single day in one local newspaper, then the national picture is likely to be very serious indeed. Yet despite this, national statistics on crime at work are not collected as a separate category. Even if they were, they would probably run up against the problem of defining 'work'—does it include incidents that happen outside or at home but are connected with work (e.g. where families are held hostage against theft from a company), incidents that happen in a company car park, and what about incidents with individuals who work from home? However, this is not an issue; statistics for crime at work are included in crime figures generally. These make depressing reading as the following illustrations indicate:

- The number of notifiable offences recorded by the police for every 100 000 of the population has increased from 5970 in 1981 to 10 400 in 1991.

- Between 1990 and 1991 offences against property rose by 17 per cent, reaching a total of 5 million.
- Between 1990 and 1991 violent crime rates rose by 6 per cent overall to reach a total of 265 000 offences.
- Perhaps most significant of all for crime at work, the criminal statistics for 1991 report that since 1990, while all types of robbery have increased, two particular types receive special mention:

  'the number of robberies of banks in which firearms were used increased by 59 per cent and of building societies 28 per cent' and, furthermore, 'injuries were caused in 18 per cent of offences where firearms were involved.'

  (Taken from *Criminal Statistics for England and Wales*, HMSO, 1991)[7]

For the reader who is interested a few other more detailed statistics on violence and crime are given in Appendix 5.

From the author's point of view it is unfortunate that the criminal statistics do not give any further detail on workplace crime. Yet from the little evidence that is available we can assume that the trends for crime at work are at least similar, and perhaps even worse than for crime generally. However, it is also worth remembering that for crimes against property and crimes by other employees (and perhaps some crimes against persons) the general criminal statistics will be underestimates of how much crime actually takes place each year. Many incidents go unreported both to employers and to the police. For a whole variety of reasons people may choose not to report a crime. For example, sometimes when an incident takes place an employee may have broken a company rule or not followed a procedure exactly. As a consequence they may see themselves as partly culpable and (if they can get away with it) decide not to report the incident. Furthermore, this tendency will be exacerbated if the employee fears that disciplinary proceedings will be invoked if their actions become known. Alternatively an employee, manager or owner of a business might simply consider it is not worth while reporting some incidents. For example, the author knows of one small suburban shop where the plate glass front door is smashed on a regular basis (i.e. 2 or 3 times a year). The incidents are now never reported as the owner has decided it is less expensive to employ a glazier to repair the damage than risk inflating his insurance premiums. It follows that where such decisions are made then whatever the proportion of crimes at work reported the criminal statistics will almost certainly be an underestimate of the underlying picture.

The specific data that are available about organizations give an equally dismal picture, for example:

- With the exception of 1992, data from the Building Societies Association[8] confirms a progressive increase in the number of robberies reported. Since 1988 the figures have been as given in Table 2.3.

Table 2.3 Number of robberies

Year	Number of robberies
1988	368
1989	646
1990	862
1991	1052
1992	940

- In 1992, BIFU (the Banking, Insurance and Finance Union) commissioned a survey of bank and building society robberies.[9] They reported that:
  - In 1991 there were 1633 armed raids on banks and building societies.
  - In London the number of attacks doubled in one year; throughout the rest of the country doubling took two years.
  - Nearly every robbery involves a weapon or threat of violence.

- In 1989 the Dixons Store Group conducted a survey of 1032 branches to assess the threat of violence to staff.[10] In the 6 months prior to the survey the company had received reports of serious threats or actual violence from only 32 branches. However, the survey showed that some 300 had experienced such incidents.
- If we broaden our area of concern to include 'lower key' events such as verbal abuse then the British Crime Survey 1988[11] highlights that:
  - 14 per cent of workers who were interviewed reported that they had been verbally abused (other than by colleagues) during the year in the course of their work; also
  - one fifth of those suffering abuse reported this had happened on more than 10 occasions.
- Probably the most comprehensive study of the costs of crime was carried out by the British Retail Consortium.[1] In their 1992-3 survey of retail crime costs in Britain they report the findings shown in Table 2.4.

Table 2.4 Survey of retail crime costs

Incident	Number of incidents	Estimated gross cost
Burglary	178 944	£331.0 million
Theft by customers	1 516 481	£516.6 million
Criminal damage	120 348	£47.1 million
Arson	3 688	£26.0 million
Robbery	14 416	£24.2 million
Physical violence	14 320	—
Threats of violence	106 181	—
Verbal abuse	298 328	—
Terrorist incidents	7 098	£52.8 million

Wherever data exist, they confirm that violence and crime at work is a major issue; it is an issue for companies through the sheer cost and inconvenience it creates; it is an issue for customers and consumers through the additional margins that must inevitably be added to the goods and services we purchase; it is an issue for society as to why so many citizens are now turning to crime; it is also an issue for victims who may become involved through no fault of their own other than as a result of the particular occupation they carry out. Yet organizations are very reluctant to publish specific information about any crime that they experience. To some extent this is understandable. For example, banks and building societies are highly unlikely to welcome publication of figures about the number of raids they have experienced or how much money has gone missing through fraud, cash machine or computer crime if they seek to present an image of being secure and reliable. To do so could be the equivalent of commercial suicide. Similarly, a Social Services Department may well start to experience recruitment problems if it became widely known that particular groups of social workers were at a high risk from abuse, threat and violence.

Obviously some organizations are more at risk than others, but unless the organization has some way of monitoring incidents that affect employees, it will be completely unaware of:

- Whether there is a problem and
- The size of the problem.

Furthermore, the experience of organizations that have carried out some form of survey has generally led to surprising results; i.e. the problem is much worse than they had ever anticipated. For example, one major petrol company was unaware of the size of the problem faced everyday by forecourt staff. This only came to light when the staff were asked. Once their views were sought it became apparent that they believed that increased customer violence was the most serious threat to their personal health and safety.

The most sensible way of finding out what problems exist and whether staff feel at risk is to ask them. This theme will be pursued further in Chapter 4; for the present it is more important to highlight a few other factors concerning the size of the problem.

These include:

- *Regional variations*   Confidential information from building societies and national retail organizations confirms that crime and violence in the financial and retail sectors is more common in London and the South East (this is in part corroborated by the BIFU illustration cited earlier). However, there is no guarantee that this trend will continue.
- *Temporal variations*   In short, the frequency of criminal incidents tends to increase around the main holiday periods, and in particular around Christmas.
- *Multiple incidents*   At first sight the raw statistics for crime and violence may give the impression of isolated incidents happening in different places and at different times. This is often not the case. Some premises, groups or individuals, for some reason, are subject to multiple incidents. For example, the author knows of one commercial premises that was subject to either robbery or attempted robbery some 25 times in a two year period. The staff involved were completely demoralized.
- *Increased levels of violence or threat*   Although there is little easily accessible data to support this point, there does seem to be a trend towards increasing levels of violence and threat to staff. For example, from press reports over the last few years firearms seem to be far more common than they were in the past. Furthermore, new types of violence seem to be creeping in. For example, incidents occur where family members are held hostage while the employee is forced to carry out some crime; or more recently there was an incident where an aggressor placed a plastic carrier bag full of explosive(?) on a building society counter and demanded money. On being given the money he walked out leaving the bomb(?) behind. The branch was immediately evacuated and the bomb disposal squad called in; they confirmed it was an explosive device.

A decade ago such incidents were unthinkable; now all one wonders is, 'What next?' Even crimes against property have reached new dimensions with the relatively new phenomenon of 'ram raids', where an entire shop doorway or frontage is smashed out by (usually) a high-powered stolen vehicle in order for those committing the crime to gain access and steal the contents of the premises. Following the raid they usually make their getaway in another (equally high-powered) stolen vehicle (some 17755 such incidents in 1992–3).[1]

Finally, although this section has attempted to concentrate on the scope of crime and violence at work it is worth remembering that the greater numbers of incidents which happen elsewhere can also have a knock-on effect at work. For example, people who are victims of, say, mugging, some sexual offence or, in some cases, burglary may need time off from work to recover and/or be unable to carry out their job satisfactorily until they have come to terms with their experience.

WHO MIGHT BE AFFECTED?

Having looked at the scale of the problem it makes sense to ask next, 'Who could be affected?' Although this is an easy question to pose, it is not as easy to answer. It depends on a combination of factors including the type of incident that has taken place, the circumstances surrounding the incident, the degree of threat/violence involved and the vulnerability of any people involved. However, with serious incidents three particular groups may need to be considered:

1. Victim(s) who were directly involved and their wider social networks, e.g. their immediate family.
2. Sometimes bystanders/onlookers to an incident.
3. Sometimes staff who should have been present but for some reason were not (perhaps through holidays, out at lunch, away ill, etc.).

Precisely how each of these groups can be affected is discussed in detail in Chapter 6. The important point to note at this stage is that although any of these people may need help following an incident, some of them could present an organization with difficulty in deciding whether or not an offer of help is appropriate (or whether any implications which flow from such a decision are desirable), e.g.:

- A small number of incidents occur where an employee's family may have been involved, e.g. in instances where family members have been held hostage or where an employee brought a child to work during school holidays or because they had a doctor's/dentist's appointment later in the day— unlikely though they may seem, such events do occur.
- Incidents occur where customers or other members of the general public are involved either as victims themselves or as witnesses or sometimes as hostages.

The difficulty is one of where to draw the line. Most organizations would recognize and accept that they have a responsibility towards their employees, even if for no other reason than their legal duty under the Health and Safety at Work Act 1974,[12] which is 'to ensure, so far as reasonably practicable, the health, safety and welfare at work of their employees'. This can extend to protecting employees from assault and attack. Equally, few organizations would baulk at providing help for the immediate family of an employee if they had been directly involved in an incident. However, extending any offer of help beyond this to members of the public is often seen by companies as more problematic. At one level it may be viewed as a very considerate gesture (and has immense 'Public Relations' value), yet it could also introduce other complications; typically these concern admission of liability in some way for what happened. I can only suggest that any company who wishes to help either customers or other members of the public should seek professional legal guidance first.

Although this chapter has sought to highlight the extent of crime and violence at work, it still has not adequately addressed the question, 'Why should an organization do anything?' Indeed, a cynic would argue that for crimes which are carried out by an external source it is more a problem for society in general. Unfortunately, this cynical view overlooks the enormous costs involved (over and above the figures mentioned earlier). Violence and crime affects both organizations and individuals and these will be the main topics for consideration in Chapters 3 and 6.

SUMMARY

- Crime at work covers a huge range of different types of criminal incidents.
- Crimes at work are now so commonplace that only the most horrific or exceptional events are reported by the media.
- Many authorities broaden their focus to include both crime and violence at work.
- It is a myth to believe that crimes directed against persons are necessarily more damaging than crimes against property.
- The definition of crime and violence which is adopted will influence the types of events that are taken into account and recorded.
- Crime and/or violence affects every occupational sector to some degree, though some groups are more at risk than others.
- It is a myth to believe that well-protected people, premises or security vehicles necessarily minimize the likelihood of an incident taking place.
- All available sources of data indicate that both crime generally and crime at work is increasing annually. In particular, in 1991 banks and building societies reported very significant increases.
- General figures for crime at work mask other important considerations, e.g. regional variations, increasing numbers of incidents prior to holiday periods, multiple incidents and a general increase in the levels of violence/threat involved.
- Crime at work affects victims (and their families), witnesses

and sometimes other staff who should have been present but for some reason were not.

- Most organizations accept a responsibility for helping staff and their immediate family who have been victimized. However, offering help to others (e.g. customers) can introduce additional complications.

3

The effects of crime and violence on an organization

INTRODUCTION

Whereas Chapter 2 highlighted the scale of crime and violence in the workplace, this chapter will look at how it can affect an organization. However, the sheer scale of attempting to discuss the effects of all types of crime would probably take up several volumes (and, in some areas, would be completely beyond the experience of the author). Of necessity, therefore, some reasonable boundary must be drawn.

It is probably fair to say that for most employers the area of greatest human concern involves abuse and violence towards employees and, at the extreme, where these become crimes against the person (i.e. primarily assault and armed raids—manslaughter, murder, sexual offences and kidnapping do happen, but, by comparison, they are much less frequent). However, although there is also an emotional impact which should not be ignored, perhaps the greatest direct cost (and inconvenience) to employers and employees alike is through crimes against property, e.g. burglary, theft (including hijacking and shoplifting), vandalism (or criminal damage) and arson. All of these have significant organizational consequences. Yet one could also argue that incidents which take place outside work can have significant organizational consequences; the author would agree. The difficulty is that somewhere a boundary must be drawn, even if it proves to be elastic. Therefore the text which follows will concentrate primarily on abuse, violence and crimes against the person. Crimes against property and crime outside work will also be considered to a lesser degree and drawn in as appropriate.

Clearly, adopting this focus excludes some important areas of crime such as fraud, cash machine and computer crime. I believe these are highly specialist areas and are probably best left to some other authority who is expert in those fields. Nevertheless, much of what will be covered in subsequent chapters concerning victims will be highly relevant for victims of even these crimes. Similarly no specific attempt will be made to address crime committed by employees, though again much of what will be discussed later will be of relevance for victims of such incidents.

Yet despite these exclusions the list of different types of incidents which remain is still considerable. Given the levels of violence and crime against persons and property which exist today, they are also probably the most important types of incidents to tackle. Indeed, within the retail sector, violence and crime perpetrated by customers constitutes the majority of all incidents.

Taking into account the boundaries imposed here, what then are the main organizational effects of violence and crime at work? Although a brief checklist of these was given in Chapter 1, each will be discussed in considerably more detail in the sections that follow.

DISRUPTION OF DAILY ACTIVITIES

One of the most obvious effects of incidents involving crimes to persons or property is the disruption involved in daily routines. Damage and/or mess may need to be cleared, and in some cases repairs carried out. Typically normal activities, trading and transactions are significantly disrupted and sometimes suspended. Often the suspension is only for an hour or two but it is not unusual for it to extend to the rest of the working day. Where a crime is a notifiable offence the police will have to be involved. Statements will need to be taken and, in some cases, forensic experts will need to be called in. In large companies the internal security and audit departments may also become involved. All this takes time, which for the company will be irreplaceable trading time. Criminal incidents (of whatever type) cost money. For busy high street operations even a few hours of lost trading can involve a considerable sum, none of which can ever be recovered.

In some organizations the disruption does not end until a few (perhaps several) days later. Subsequent police, internal security and/or audit inquiries can introduce further interruptions for both management and staff alike.

With abuse and verbal aggression or threat, the organizational effects may be less obvious. Some employees (in particular those who have been trained to manage abuse and threat) are able to deal with such incidents effectively without any disruption to normal activities. For them 'it is all in a day's work'. However, many employees are not trained in this way and as a consequence such incidents can lead to them feeling abused or the butt-end of someone else's mistakes or negligence. This can in turn lead to abrupt or terse behaviour with other people (often other customers) who are dealt with subsequently. In other instances, being on the receiving end of abusive behaviour can also lead to anger or distress. In situations where abuse is repetitious it may lead to a defensive (often hostile) atmosphere. From an organizational point of view, this type of behaviour is contrary to the 'care for the customer' image which nowadays most companies wish to project. The quality of service will deteriorate and in the longer term this is likely to reflect in poorer business performance.

DIRECT COSTS OF MONEY, GOODS OR INFORMATION STOLEN

When an incident involves robbery, burglary, hijacking or other forms of theft, the organization will also have to take into account any money, goods or information stolen. As far as money and goods are concerned, these are probably the most easily measurable aspect of crime. As we saw in the last chapter, the sums involved in the retail sector alone are huge. As a consequence many organizations have introduced procedures and practices to keep losses to a minimum, e.g. lower till limits, electronic security tagging of goods, more highly visible security guards, sophisticated video systems, vehicle tracking devices, bullet resistant screens, etc. Once again, in 1992–3 the retail sector spent some £370 million on crime prevention. Nevertheless, despite all of this the direct costs of losses through crime are still huge. However, even where any losses are covered by some form of insurance (as will be mentioned later) there are still adverse consequences for the company.

Measuring the cost of information loss is far more difficult and might not even be noticed by a company. Modern small computer disks can hold enormous amounts of information and are very easy to conceal.

REPAIR AND REPLACEMENT COSTS

Although most incidents involve little if any damage to property or equipment, this is not always the case. Sometimes the damage involved is considerable; equipment may be smashed; telephones ripped out or broken; safes tampered with; doors and locks broken; in extreme cases, even the fabric of the building may be destroyed. Indeed burglary nearly always involves damage to property and, as the following case studies illustrate, this can sometimes prevent any further business or trading until repairs are carried out or other temporary accommodation is found.

Case Study 3.1

During the early hours of the morning a gang of villains reversed a stolen lorry into the back wall of a small suburban Post Office. Under the impact of the vehicle the wall crumbled, leaving open access to the safe in the back office. Within a couple of minutes the safe had been hooked up to the lorry and was dragged off to a nearby car park. Although the thieves failed to open the safe, the office was put out of action completely for several days. This in turn disrupted the entire community as the next nearest office was a couple of miles away. Temporary premises were opened again within two weeks but the original building remained out of action for several months while major structural repairs were carried out.

Case Study 3.2

In order to avoid tripping window or door-operated alarm switches, a small group of burglars broke into a high street clothing store by climbing on to the roof and removing sections of roofing. Having gained access into the roof space above the shop, they dropped into the premises below by breaking down the ceiling.

When the staff opened up for business the following morning, not only had all the more expensive items been stolen but also the shop itself looked like a demolition site. Any further trading was impossible until the external roof had been patched up and the ceiling in the shop repaired. The cost of the incident was greatly in excess of simply the items that were stolen.

INFLATION OF INSURANCE PREMIUMS

The sums of money paid out by insurance companies as a result of workplace crime are enormous. For example, according to the Association of British Insurers[13] the sums paid out as a result of commercial theft over the last three years are as follows:

1990—£232.9 million
1991—£316.6 million
1992—£276.2 million

The decrease from 1991 to 1992 is interesting, given that theft in general increased over the same period. Furthermore, whether the decrease will be sustained in 1993 has yet to be seen. Nevertheless, despite this, the actual sums of money involved are considerable and have to be reflected in the cost of premiums. Unfortunately the way premiums for commercial risk are assessed is actually quite complicated and depends on a whole variety of factors, e.g. size of business, type of business, type of risk cover involved, etc. Consequently, it would be meaningless to attempt to give an overall figure for the levels of increase over the past few years as they differ widely from one situation to the next. However, the range of annual increases between 1990 and 1993 has varied from remaining the same (in a small number of cases) to 25 per cent (or more).

Furthermore, where an individual company makes repetitive claims then the insurance company will inevitably impose additional 'penalty' premiums or, in the longer term, become reluctant to accept the risk. In effect the company will become a liability and simply uninsurable.

It is also worth reflecting on the fact that increasing insurance premiums to cover losses through crime are carried (to some extent) by all companies, not just those who have been the victim of crime. In a sense, therefore, all companies pay towards the cost of crime.

SICKNESS ABSENCE COSTS

In general this is not as great a cost as might be imagined. While it is true that some staff do take time off after an incident (either at work or elsewhere), most do not. From confidential surveys carried out in organizations, typically only 10 to 15 per cent of victims take any time off at all. However, if this is not acknowledged by the organization then victims may feel they have to lie about the reason for their absence. In companies that do not have a policy which permits time off with pay it is not unusual to find that time off is taken either as sick leave (using a spurious reason) or as annual leave. Indeed, it is often the case that staff simply take time off and do not have a clue as to how it is recorded.

This does seem to indicate that some form of policy may be needed with regard to time off, but again this is not as simple as it first appears. On the one hand acknowledging that some people may need time off (without financial penalty) seems to be very important. At the other extreme, such a policy should not encourage staff to take time off if they do not need it. To do so will increase the organizational costs of crime unnecessarily. Somewhere a balance has to be drawn between the two. However, as this concerns how an organization responds to incidents further discussion will be left until later.

Before closing this section a few additional points about absence need to be highlighted:

- The reason for people needing time off is very often the result of their psychological reaction rather than any physical injury. In this respect the following myth is particularly relevant.

'The amount of time off which people will need following an incident is directly related to how much physical injury they suffer.'

This is simply not true. Some people suffer terribly from incidents which others can take in their stride; there is no simple relationship between injury and suffering. As will be repeated again later, the wide range of responses which different people experience *must be accepted as normal.*

- Although the need for time off work is usually associated with violence or crime against the person (e.g. assault and armed raids), sometimes crime against property can have equally disturbing consequences for the people involved.
- Quite often victims find the need for time off is greatest after a

delay. It is as if they tried to cope with their reaction to the incident by carrying on as normal, but then the effects became too great and a short break away from the scene of the incident became necessary. In the author's experience this type of delayed reaction is fairly common.

- While generally the level of absence following an incident is low, there are startling exceptions. Some victims are so badly affected that they are absent from work for very lengthy periods (i.e. 100 days plus) and indeed some never return.

RELIEF STAFF COSTS

Over the last few years most organizations have scrutinized staffing levels and where necessary reduced them to the bare minimum. As a result the staff who remain have little flexibility to cover any situations where one (or more) of them are absent. Consequently when staff are absent, the work they would usually have carried out is either not done or is sometimes given to colleagues (perhaps involving overtime or some other premium payment), or relief staff are drawn in to make up for the absence of regular staff. Clearly all of these options involve additional cost, either directly or indirectly, which the organization must fund.

LOWER STAFF MORALE AND HIGHER LEVELS OF STRESS

There is no doubt that violent incidents and crime in general affect staff. This is one of the hidden costs of violence and crime in the workplace. Typically it is greater in situations which are at risk from incidents against the person (though yet again there are exceptions). The survey carried out by BIFU[9] reported that staff involved in criminal incidents sometimes experience a number of lasting effects, e.g.:

- 26 per cent are still afraid or nervous.

- 25 per cent are unsettled or uneasy.
- 34 per cent are feeling angry.
- 37 per cent are unable to trust people.
- 22 per cent are somewhat afraid to work at the counter (presumably where the incident took place).
- 19 per cent do not want to be alone.

BIFU also reported other specific longer term effects including feeling wary, suspicious (especially of customers), more tense, fear and nervousness. The author would agree and further point out that all of these reactions are magnified when staff are repeatedly exposed to threat, violence and/or crime (particularly if the organization refuses to look at the problem or offer any help).

For the organization all of this equates to increased stress for staff who have been, or may be, involved in other incidents in the future. Everyone is aware that violence and crime will not disappear overnight. Unless some form of action is taken, then in high-risk situations stress will be high and morale low. Staff will no longer trust customers, the organization, and in some cases their fellow colleagues. This will inevitably lead to poorer performance which, in simple commercial terms, costs money (and sometimes a great deal of money).

REQUESTS FOR TRANSFER AND/OR INCREASED STAFF TURNOVER

Victims of crime often engage in avoidance behaviour as a way of coping, i.e. they try to find ways of avoiding the situation where the incident occurred. At work this can manifest in a number of ways, e.g.:

- Reluctance to return to their normal work station. They will try to obtain a transfer to another job (usually one which they perceive as much less at risk from any future incident).
- In larger organizations which have a network of outlets/offices staff may be reluctant to return to the premises where the

incident occurred. They may try to obtain a transfer to a different office which they perceive as being less at risk.

- Reluctance to return to work for the organization at all. Furthermore, as will be highlighted in Chapter 6, the pressure for victims to leave high-risk jobs may be made worse by family reactions. These often involve vehement anger that a partner/son/daughter has been put at risk and often the organization will be seen as the culprit for not providing better protection.

Case Study 3.3

'When I told him what had happened he just flipped. I don't think I've ever seen him so angry before. I got even more upset. He just kept going on about why had I been put in such a position—why wasn't more protection provided—that I should get another job rather than end up as a corpse.

I know he meant well, but it didn't help with him going on that way.'

Again, all of these behaviours will be exacerbated where staff feel the organization is not concerned about the risks to which they are exposed.

RECRUITMENT DIFFICULTIES

Difficulty with recruitment is the next stage on from transfer requests and staff leaving. Not only will staff wish to be transferred out of 'at risk' offices but other staff who know of an office's reputation will be reluctant to take their place. Although external recruitment of replacement staff may be fairly easy during times of high unemployment, people may become far more cautious about putting themselves at risk when unemployment figures are lower.

SUMMARY

- Criminal incidents disrupt normal daily activities—sometimes only briefly, but sometimes for much longer.

- Despite highly sophisticated security systems for preventing crime, the direct cost of losses through theft are still very large.
- Damage to property or equipment during incidents can range from none to very serious structural damage requiring major repair work.
- The sums of money paid out by insurance companies as a result of crime are huge; consequently, this is reflected in the levels of premiums paid by companies.
- The costs of sickness absence following violence and crime are generally not excessive; however, there are startling exceptions.
- Staff who are exposed to high-risk situations often experience high stress and low morale.
- Repetitious crime may well lead to staff requesting transfers to other jobs/offices or in a few cases leaving altogether. In some circumstances replacing them may prove difficult.

4

Monitoring incidents

INTRODUCTION

We saw in Chapter 2 that violence and crime affects many organizations, yet, surprisingly, relatively few have any procedure in place for monitoring the extent of incidents. It follows that where a company has no procedure then inevitably it will have no way of knowing with any certainty where a problem exists. Furthermore, in companies where there is a problem they will not know the scale of the problem, what kind of incidents are affecting staff or how best to introduce any measures to keep incidents to a minimum. Indeed, it is worth reflecting on the statement in Chapter 2 that where companies have carried out some form of survey with staff, they have generally been surprised by the results; the problem is often much worse than they had ever anticipated. Unless violence and crime is very obvious (as with armed raids and shoplifting) the vast majority of incidents (particularly those which involve abuse or verbal aggression) are rarely reported. Note that even where a company has an incident procedure it is still worth checking:

1. Whether the procedure is up to date with any changes in the current pattern of crime and violence.
2. Whether the procedure is merely cosmetic or actually used.
3. Whether the range of incidents covered is comprehensive.

Where there is no procedure then the easiest way to find out if a problem exists is to ask the staff who may be at risk.

CARRYING OUT A STAFF SURVEY

Carrying out a staff survey may sound like quite a formidable task; however, this need not be the case. There are many ways for an organization to collect information from employees, e.g.:

- Through the management chain. First line managers or supervisors can be requested to collect information on violence and crime from their immediate work groups. If the organization already has in place some form of management communication system like 'team briefing' or 'quality circles' these could be an ideal forum for data collection. Alternatively, it may be possible to use other existing types of staff meeting, e.g. perhaps part of a staff training session.
- By holding a series of specific meetings with staff to establish their views, or, in larger organizations, meeting with representative samples of staff.
- In organizations where the majority of staff belong to a trade union or staff association (assuming relationships with them are cordial), then information gathering might be possible through the union structure of staff representatives. In the author's experience, typically trade unions are very supportive of any initiative which is about helping their membership. They can be a very powerful ally, though they may be wary if they suspect that a survey is to be used to collect information to highlight and discipline employees who have not followed procedures to the letter. However, it must be accepted that in some companies this type of approach would be simply unthinkable.
- By carrying out a confidential questionnaire survey with staff in general or with a representative sample.

Obviously there are also many other variations that could be chosen instead, depending on the size and type of company, the resources available, etc. The crucial point is that employees are consulted and their point of view taken into account.

However, before embarking on any survey or information

gathering exercise, perhaps we should go back a step and think through what information needs to be gathered and what questions to ask. This brings us back to the point mentioned in Chapter 2, that the way we define 'crime', 'violence' or 'abuse' will influence what type of questions are asked and what is considered important in any information given in reply. For example, to focus too tightly on 'crime' may well ignore abuse and verbal aggression (which falls short of actual crime but may be far more prevalent and of widespread concern). Equally, to focus on violence could ignore incidents where employees are not directly involved (e.g. burglary), yet for some people even these incidents can be quite distressing (both at work and elsewhere).

The only sound advice seems to be to select the questions which, from an organizational point of view, need to be asked and then listen to the replies—*hear* what is said. Listen to the replies openly rather than selectively (i.e. by discounting what is not within the area the question was intended to explore). Try to hear what people are really saying without allowing preconceptions to act as a filter. After all, most of us (the author included) can be masters of selective listening.

When considering what types of questions could be important, the following checklist of survey questions may be of help:

- What types of incidents affect staff?
- How severely would they rate any incidents?
- How are they affected?
- What is the frequency of incidents (e.g. over the last 6 or 12 months)?
- Who or what helped/hindered?
- Were the police involved?
- Was any absence involved?
- Were any customers/members of the public involved?
- What could the organization do to help?

Some of these questions ask for quite sensitive information in reply. Therefore it is important to consider who or what department is asking the questions (and will have sight of any conclusions). Replies given to a manager or supervisor may be very different to replies given to personnel or security staff, even though the questions may be the same.

If a company is really seeking an honest response from staff then whoever asks the questions needs to have the trust and respect of staff. Ideally any information gathered in the survey will be treated confidentially. The concern of the organization is to establish if there is a problem, not identify 'who said what'. It does make sense, therefore, to consider who or what department is likely to be perceived by staff as most trustworthy. In large organizations violence and crime often involves several different groups, any one of which could have a legitimate reason for conducting a survey, e.g.:

- Managers and supervisors
- Personnel/human resources
- Security
- Health and safety
- Occupational health
- Welfare
- Legal department
- Senior managers/board members

Obviously in smaller companies the choice will be more restricted. However, in all but the smallest of organizations there should be at least a few options from which to choose.

Once the survey has been carried out the results will need to be collated into a form suitable for aiding decision making. Again this can have consequences for how the survey is carried out. It is very easy to identify a great many facets of the problem on which it would be interesting to collect information. However, this may lead to so much data that only a statistician would be able to unravel what aspects are significant. Hence, it is important to keep data collection in perspective. Generally its purpose is to aid and enable decision making, not provide the substance for an academic thesis.

Once complete, the survey results should give a clear picture of whether there is a problem, and if so it should also give an indication of:

- The scale and size of the problem
- What kind of incidents concern employees
- The range of effects on employees
- Some approximation of the frequency of incidents

The organization is then left with a decision about what to do next. In this respect it is worth remembering that simply carrying out a survey will start to communicate to employees the fact that management are concerned about what is happening. However, where there is a problem it can also set up an expectation that some form of action will be taken as a result. In the first instance this usually means:

- Setting up an ongoing monitoring and information system
- Where possible attempting to do something to minimize incidents

How to set up a monitoring system will be dealt with in the next section. However, action to minimize incidents will be addressed separately in Chapter 5.

INTRODUCING A MONITORING AND INFORMATION SYSTEM

Some form of monitoring and management information system is essential in order to provide the organization with accurate information on incidents that take place. However, up until now it has been assumed that in some nebulous way the organization will take responsibility for ensuring this happens. In most companies the concept of a corporate body taking action is a nonsense. What must happen is that some individual, group or department accepts responsibility for making sure that the issue is pursued. Organizational action comes about as a result of one or more people deciding to champion a cause or particular line of action.

With respect to violence and crime, in hierarchical organizations it generally follows that the more senior the person (or group) raising the issue, the more quickly any action will be taken.

What is clear is that no matter where the ball starts rolling (e.g. security, personnel/human resources, training or occupational health, etc.) setting up a monitoring system and carrying out any subsequent action will require a coordinator or coordinating group. Furthermore, as violence and crime impacts across several departments, this body will need to have sufficient authority to be able to influence all of the departments involved. It would be folly to have, say, personnel and security following one line of action while occupational health decides to 'do its own thing'. Similarly, in large national organizations with offices and outlets spread all over the country, central coordination will be needed to avoid unnecessary regional variations.

Very large organizations sometimes make the role of coordinator a full-time post (e.g. see Chapter 11), though clearly in smaller companies this will be neither possible nor necessary. The role can be satisfactorily carried out as part of the duties of one or more other appropriate specialists (often in either personnel/human resources or security). However, it is worth stressing again that whoever carries out the coordinating role *must* have authority (either themselves or through senior management) to implement organizational change. To be effective the coordinating body will need to become a fulcrum for organizational development. Addressing violence and crime at work is much more than simply starting to take note of when and where incidents occur; it often involves cultural change as well.

Normally the coordinating body would design and implement a monitoring system. However, in order to do this they will have to decide what type of incidents need recording and what can be ignored. Clearly, as was mentioned in Chapter 2, there is no simple answer to this; what is acceptable behaviour in one setting will be completely unacceptable in another. For example, the author recalls interviews with two headmasters concerning teenage abuse and violence towards teachers. One Head took the position that verbal aggression and abuse towards teachers was common-place and behaviour which staff should be able to manage without reference to any more senior level. However, the other viewed verbal aggression and abuse of teachers as behaviour which could (and did) result in the pupil being expelled from the school. In his view acceptable behaviour should never include aggression or abuse of others. Similarly, in commercial settings, staff who work at a complaints desk or complaints phone-line may accept verbal aggression, occasionally being spat at and abused as part of a normal day at work, whereas others most certainly would not.

Generally there is little disagreement over the need to record more serious and criminal events; the difficulties usually arise over verbal incidents. Clearly, in deciding what to do the coordinating body will need to use its judgement about what is reasonable to expect from staff.

Having decided what incidents to monitor, the next step usually involves designing some method for recording them. This may be a paper incident record form or an electronic IT equivalent. Either way the coordinating body will need to decide precisely what information needs to be collected about incidents. This could include:

- The time, place, day and date of the incident
- A brief description of what happened
- Who was involved
- Any weapons used
- Any injuries or fatalities sustained
- Any witnesses present
- Any goods, equipment, money or information stolen
- Details of the assailants

The important point to remember is that any record should be kept as simple as possible. As we will see in Chapter 6, after some incidents people may feel badly shaken, perhaps emotionally upset and unable to think straight. Having to complete even the most simple document or record can be a real struggle. Furthermore, the one universal complaint from staff in practically all organizations is 'too much paperwork'. Unnecessarily long or complicated forms will merely fuel their complaint still further; simplicity must be the order of the day. An illustration incident report form is given in Figure 4.1.

Once the procedure has been approved, it will then need to be introduced to the managers and staff who will have to use it. Again there are several options for how it could be launched, these include:

- Issuing a standing order or permanent instruction to the effect that the procedure will be in operation and carried out fully from a particular date. This will probably need coupling with some form of explanatory letter or memo giving details about the procedure itself, why it has been introduced, how it is envisaged it will work and how the information will be used. However, although this type of organizational practice still exists, it is generally the least satisfactory way of introducing any new procedure. It offers no opportunity for discussion, clarification or explanation of any points of concern.
- As with carrying out a survey, a second option is to use existing meeting structures. In this respect organizations which use 'team briefing', 'quality circles', regular staff training sessions or regular staff meetings are at a real advantage. It should be relatively easy to ensure the new procedure is placed on their agenda or in their programme of topics to be covered.
- Holding a series of dedicated meetings with staff to explain the procedure, why it is being introduced, what it seeks to achieve and, most important of all, how employees will benefit as a result. In large diverse organizations it would simply not be possible for the coordinator or members of the coordinating team to visit every single work group or location and it may be necessary to ask for help from some other section (e.g. training and development). Obviously, organizationally this is the most expensive option. However, it will invariably be far more effective than simply sending out written instructions.

Once the procedure has been up and running for some time

INCIDENT REPORT

Date of incident......................... Time.............. Day of week..............
Address where incident took place...
....

Employees directly involved   Job/Grade

....

....

....

What happened? Please give a brief description of the incident and the events leading up to it (if it would help, please draw a sketch map on the other side of the page).

....

....

....

What was the outcome? Please give details of any injuries, physical or verbal abuse, damage to property, personal belongings or any equipment.

....

....

....

Description of assailants, e.g. male/female, height, clothing, hair, skin or eye colour, any distinguishing features, scars, marks or behaviour.

....

....

Witnesses .... Address...

....

....

Any other relevant information?

....

....

Thank you for your help

Figure 4.1   Illustration incident record form

the coordinator or coordinating body should be able to start to build up an accurate picture of where and when violence and crime is occurring within the organization, together with its effects on both the organization and the people involved. Careful analysis might start to reveal important patterns:

- Who is most at risk
- Common causes
- Common locations
- Particular times of the day or week which are high risk (e.g. just before closing time for many shops and offices)

Findings such as these could have important implications for highlighting when and where preventative measures can be taken. Clearly, where possible, prevention is far more desirable than having to deal with the consequences afterwards. Therefore, it makes a great deal of sense to spend at least a little time looking at prevention.

However, before doing this there is one final point worth highlighting about monitoring procedures. Patterns of violence and crime do change over time; it is therefore important that any monitoring procedure does not become ossified and out of touch. From time to time it is important to check whether the procedure continues to be comprehensive and actually is keeping up with any changes that take place.

SUMMARY

- Although violence and crime is common in many organizations, relatively few have any procedure for monitoring incidents.
- Even where a company has a procedure it is worth checking whether it is comprehensive, up to date and actually used.
- Before any survey is carried out it is important to think through how the survey will be implemented, what questions will be asked and who will do the asking.

- Once completed, the survey should give a clear indication if a problem exists, and, if so, the scale, size and extent of the problem.
- Setting up a monitoring system will require either an individual or group to act as a central coordinator or coordinating group.
- Once established, the coordinator/coordinating group will have to decide what type of incidents are recorded together with some mechanism for recording them.
- Any mechanism for recording incidents must be kept simple.
- Analysis of the data gathered from monitoring incidents can often highlight important areas where preventative measures can be taken.

Minimizing incidents

PREVENTATIVE MEASURES

Effective measures for preventing violence and crime at work are highly organization specific. They will depend on a variety of factors, such as:

- The type of organization
- What/who is at risk
- The location and layout of the premises
- The nature of the occupations at risk
- Hours of operation etc.

With violence and crime there are no ready-made answers; every organization, occupation and location will need to be assessed individually. However, as early as 1981, at their annual conference, the TUC identified a range of common actions that could help minimize the risk of violence to staff.[14] They included:

- Changing the job to give less face-to-face contact with the public. For example, introducing automatic ticket dispensers/ collectors and cash machines. However, care must be taken to ensure that such measures do not increase the risks of violence to members of the general public because there are no visible staff.
- As far as possible moving away from any cash transactions. Using cheques, credit cards or tokens instead of cash is likely to make robbery less attractive. For example, some milk delivery staff now operate a token system.
- Providing training for employees, either to give them more

knowledge and confidence in their particular jobs or to enable them to deal with aggression generally, by spotting the early signs and avoiding or coping with it. This will be examined in more detail in the next section.

- Segregating staff from the public by putting protective screens around them, as in some banks, social security offices and bus drivers' cabs.
- Reviewing staffing arrangements to avoid, as far as possible, staff working alone in high-risk situations.
- Improving communication and warning systems to enable staff to call for help quickly and easily.

More recently, the Health and Safety Executive[4] have added a few more:

- Checking the credentials of 'clients' and if possible the place and arrangements for meetings away from the office. This is standard practice now for some estate agents.
- Making sure that staff can get home safely. The threat of violence does not stop when work has ended. The Health and Safety at Work Act requires employers to protect employees only while they are at work, but all good employers will take further steps where necessary. For example, if staff have to work late, arrangements should be made for them to be able to park their cars in a safe area or have door-to-door transport home provided.
- Changing the layout of public waiting areas. Better seating, decor, lighting and more regular information about delays have helped stop tension building up in some hospital waiting rooms, housing departments and benefit offices.
- Using wider counters, and raising the height of the floor on the staff side of the counter to give staff more protection. Some pubs have also done this.
- Installing video cameras or alarm buttons; on buses, cameras have protected staff and reduced vandalism and graffiti.
- Using 'coded' security locks on doors to keep the public out of staff areas.

Additionally, it may also be worth mentioning that there is some evidence that the 'open-plan' layout of many recently refurbished banks and building societies does lead to a reduction in the number of incidents. The complexity of the layout seems to require more complicated planning for a robbery and hence acts as a deterrent.

If the coordinator or coordinating body is also charged with making recommendations for preventing incidents, they would be well advised to draw on as much help as possible. Although this is primarily the domain of the security expert, it is worth remembering that employees are more likely to be committed to new security measures if they have been able to help design and implement them. Furthermore, trade unions and safety representatives may also be able to offer valuable ideas. They can make a very positive contribution.

The more that prevention of violence and crime can be seen as a collaborative venture the better. It is not just a problem for the organization; it also involves individual employees, the unions and associations that represent them, and specialist departments like security and health and safety. They all have a part to play.

It is also worth remembering that all measures to minimize or prevent incidents will have to be balanced against possible interference with the business in other ways. For example, bank and building societies wish to remain secure against robbery and burglary; however, they also need to present an approachable 'user friendly' image. Sometimes these two needs may come into conflict. An illustration of this is found in the debate among bank and building society staff over bullet-resistant or rising screens. Some staff believe they are essential for personal protection, whereas others argue that they are not necessary and that they interfere with normal customer relations. Although rare, they further point out that the presence of screens can lead to staff who are outside of any screened area or customers being held hostage. Yet again, even in the area of prevention, there are no easy answers.

To close this section it is worth re-emphasizing the point that many workplace incidents are not sufficiently serious to be defined as crimes but they do involve verbal aggression and abuse (and sometimes racial, sexual and homophobic abuse). Many employees find that having to put up with such behaviour is demotivating, humiliating and wearing. Indeed, in some occupations, being on the receiving end of aggression or abuse is practically inevitable, e.g. staff who deal regularly with customer complaints. In cases like these perhaps the most helpful preventative measure a company can take is to provide training in early identification and how to manage aggression and abuse. However, before launching into the detail of how to manage aggression and abuse it is important to point out that some incidents will involve abuse of one employee by another. Where such incidents are ignored or not dealt with satisfactorily by management, then any attempt to provide training on managing aggression by outsiders is likely to fail.

MANAGING AGGRESSION AND ABUSE

Providing training to manage aggression and abuse is about helping employees:

1. Identify the early signs of aggression and abuse and
2. Either take action to avoid the aggression and abuse or cope with the situation.

However, before discussing either of these points in any detail, it is worth taking a step backwards and asking why aggressive or abusive incidents arise. Nowadays there are many situations where people start to become frustrated, angry and sometimes violent. They include:

- *Being kept waiting* Probably every reader of this text will have been kept waiting unnecessarily on many occasions, e.g. a late train, doctor's and dentist's waiting rooms, traffic jams, delays at airports, inefficient organizations, etc.—the causes are legion. When trapped in such situations some people become very angry. Where this is not acknowledged and dealt with, it sometimes leads to abusive or even violent outbursts towards anyone who represents the organization perceived to be at fault.

- *Unhelpful staff attitudes* Again no doubt most readers will have come up against employees in all types of organizations (both public and private) who are unhelpful, brusque and sometimes downright rude. Indeed, quite recently I recall visiting the enquiry office of a government department in an attempt to clarify a financial question. The answer given was both dismissive and unhelpful. Although this particular incident did not lead to an aggressive incident, for some people such behaviour seems to invite aggression. 'Well, they deserved it!' is a comment often made in defence of violent actions.

  While abuse and violence cannot be condoned, it is a fact that where employees show little sympathy or understanding for people, then it is inevitable that, sooner or later, tempers will flare. Furthermore, when people do become angry, then staff who are unskilled in helping them calm down will make the situation even worse and eventually become victims themselves.

- *Bureaucracy and red tape* Even today, in many organizations bureaucracy and red tape are still a way of life. Yet for customers, and sometimes employees, it can create frustration and irritation. Being passed from one department to another, having to fill in mindless forms and senseless requisitions (often in triplicate) can all add up to a recipe for aggression and violence.

- *Invasion of privacy* In order to obtain benefits or other forms of grant, aid or income supplement, people may have to put up with questioning which they consider intrusive. If badly handled this can be perceived as demeaning or humiliating. Once again, in some instances this can lead to aggression and violence.

- *Feeling aggrieved* Many organizational situations can lead to people feeling aggrieved, sometimes spilling over into anger and violence, e.g. employees who have been bypassed for promotion, or treated unfairly in some way; customers who believe they have received shoddy goods or service.
- *Alcohol* The link between alcohol and violence is now well established. Employees or customers who are under the effects of alcohol are far more likely to resort to aggression and violence as a way of resolving any disagreement.

Employees who work in occupations or organizations where any of these factors are present are much more likely to experience aggression, abuse and violence. However, aggression and violence generally do not happen without warning. Very few people engage in gratuitous violence (it must be accepted that a few do, but they are a minority). More often there is a build-up of feelings over a short period of time which culminate in aggression and violence. The key is being able to recognize the build-up and either take action to defuse the situation or escape before a crisis point is reached.

What then are the indicators that signal that someone is becoming frustrated and angry (before they reach the point of overt aggression)? The following checklist of signals that indicate increasing frustration, tension and anger may be of value:

- Increasingly tense body language, e.g. clenched jaw, flared nostrils, clenched fists, finger pointing, desk thumping
- Increased rate of breathing
- Head shaking, overt disagreement, either avoiding eye contact or sometimes a fixed hostile stare
- Noticeable change in speaking voice, e.g. slowing down and more insistent or speeding up, and perhaps also a change in voice level, either increasing or decreasing in volume
- Increasing use of statements or replies starting with 'Yes but . . .'
- Repetition of the same point or complaint
- Swearing, using personally insulting language or name calling

- The general atmosphere/tenor of the interaction becoming more tense

Where employees have to confront customers or others (e.g. members of the public, other employees, etc.) displaying such behaviour, there is a real possibility that the situation will escalate into overt aggression and sometimes violence. Furthermore, the longer the situation continues the more likely it is that aggression and violence will result.

However, aggression can often be defused by appropriate behaviour from any employee who is involved. Before discussing these techniques in any detail it is worth thinking through how you would react to aggression. The following exercise may help.

Exercise 5.1

Imagine you are in a dialogue with a customer (or other employee) over a complaint or grievance which they feel strongly about. To your surprise, as the dialogue proceeds you become aware that they are becoming increasingly frustrated and are starting to show signs of aggression.

On a separate sheet of paper write down how you would deal with the situation. When you have finished compare your approach with the reactions outlined in the discussion below.

When confronted with someone who is angry people respond in a variety of different ways. One common reaction is to meet aggression with aggression. Typically this results in one of three outcomes: a 'stand-off' (where both parties 'lock horns', but in some unspoken way agree not to engage in further battle), eventual capitulation by one side or the other or an escalation of aggression into outright violence. Another response is to give in immediately at the first sign of any hostility, allowing the aggressor to have the upper hand.

Unfortunately none of these responses leads to a satisfactory resolution of the complaint (or grievance). Either the customer (or other employee) ends up feeling even more aggrieved or humiliated, or the employee ends up feeling similarly trodden down. Both are variations of a win–lose outcome. The only difference is in who ends up as the winner and who ends up as the loser.

If meeting aggression with aggression and giving way immediately do not lead to a satisfactory outcome, then what does? The key to managing aggression successfully starts with understanding in more detail what happens inside the aggressor. Typically, frustration and anger start to build up because the aggressor feels, for one reason or another, that their complaint or grievance is not being heard or dealt with satisfactorily. However, as their feelings become more intense the aggressor will also become increasingly confused, unable to think logically and unable to listen effectively. Therefore, there is no point in an employee simply reiterating company policy, defending the company's position or making excuses. Whatever they say is unlikely to be heard (or at best heard only selectively). The primary strategy for managing aggression must start by demonstrating to the aggressor that they are being heard, understood and taken seriously. This means:

1. Staying calm and in control. If both parties are drawn into a disagreement and both become frustrated and angry then thinking and listening is likely to be ineffective on both sides. In no time at all what started as a minor issue can become a source of vehement aggression. Staying calm and in control must be the first priority.
2. Adopting an open non-aggressive body posture. Non-verbal signals often speak louder than words. In any disagreement, even if the language used is meant to convey understanding it can be totally undermined by incongruent body language.
3. Establishing eye contact (but not a fixed stare) and using affirmative para-verbal signals, e.g. 'uh-huh'.
4. Listening to what is being said and acknowledging that the content has been heard. There are two central techniques that can be used here:
   (a) By reflecting back, paraphrasing or summarizing the content of the disagreement or complaint. This has the

effect of confirming that whatever an aggressor has said has been heard and understood.

(b) Equally powerful is to use similar language to an aggressor. For example, some people seem to use predominantly visual language:
  — Can you *see* what I mean?
  — Is that *clear*?
  — Can you shed any *light* on this?
  — You don't *appear* to understand.

Alternatively, others may use auditory language:
  — You just don't *hear* what I'm saying.
  — That *rings* a bell.
  — That *sounds* about right.
  — You're just not *listening* to me.

Finally, yet other people use mainly kinaesthetic language:
  — You've no *feeling* for this.
  — That really *grates*.
  — I *feel uneasy* about that.

Using similar language then becomes a case of listening for which type of words the aggressor uses and then using similar words in response, i.e. visual language to match visual statements, auditory language to match auditory statements, etc.

(Note that although both of these techniques may seem very simple when written as words on a page, they do require considerable skill and practice in order to use them effectively.)

5. Using the assertiveness technique of 'negative enquiry' to make sure the grievance or complaint has been fully explored. In brief, this involves, firstly, inviting the other person to state their grievance, complaint or problem, and then reflecting back what they have said to check understanding. Once understanding has been confirmed, they should be asked whether there is anything further. If necessary the whole process should be repeated again and again. Perhaps the easiest way to describe this technique is through an illustration of an incident between a customer and an employee:

CUSTOMER   I'm absolutely fed up with you lot. Call yourself a service company, you haven't a clue.

EMPLOYEE   I can see you're feeling pretty angry. However, could you tell me what the problem is and I will do my best to help?

CUSTOMER   Angry! Anyone would be angry if they were treated like I've been.

EMPLOYEE   Yes?

CUSTOMER   One of your service engineers came to repair my washer two weeks ago. He said it would need a spare part and would ring to let me know when he was coming back. He didn't and every time I've rung your office since then I've just been fobbed off.

EMPLOYEE   I see, so one of our engineers tried to repair your washer. He found it needed a part but failed to contact you as he had promised. Since then you feel your enquiries have not been taken seriously. Is that right?

CUSTOMER   Yes, wouldn't you be angry?

EMPLOYEE   I see, tell me, is there anything else?

CUSTOMER   Yes, to make matters worse, when I was put through to your service department, whoever I spoke to was really rude. That's what prompted me to come here myself.

EMPLOYEE   So, when you spoke with our service department you feel you were treated badly. Have I got that right?

CUSTOMER   Yes.

EMPLOYEE   Is there anything else?

CUSTOMER   Yes, and ....

The purpose of negative enquiry is to flush out the whole issue. At every stage the employee acknowledges what the customer has said (without saying whether they agree or disagree), but also checks out whether there is anything else. Often this brings to light other aspects of the issue which previously were not voiced. However, as the whole process continues, it generally has the effect of calming the other person down. Although the complaint or grievance is not yet settled, at least the aggrieved party will feel that they have been heard and taken seriously. Furthermore, once they have talked through their frustrations they will usually be in a much more receptive frame of mind to listen to explanations, apologies or any relevant company procedure.

Although carrying out these actions will defuse the majority of potentially aggressive situations, they will not work in every case. In a minority of incidents some people will become aggressive and violent regardless of what employees say or do. It makes sense, therefore, for employees who are at risk to have some other strategy for dealing with situations where they feel personally in danger of being harmed. This could include:

- A concealed panic or alarm switch (or personal alarm) to enable assistance to be summoned very rapidly. If an organization chooses to use this idea then it is also worth pointing out that, in an emergency, assistance may be needed very quickly indeed; any delay could be too late.

- Ensuring that employees do not have to work alone in high-risk situations or, alternatively, where this is not possible, having a procedure whereby their safety can be either continuously monitored or checked at frequent intervals.

- Easy access to an escape route so that an employee can either walk away or safely escape from any immediate threat. However, although this will guarantee the safety of the employee, it is also likely to infuriate any aggressor. As a consequence they may do extensive damage to any property or equipment that is nearby.

Although this chapter has concentrated on minimizing and managing incidents at work, it must also be accepted that where individuals are motivated by criminal intent then incidents are inevitable. There is no level or type of preventative measure or action that will deter all crime. Acknowledging this as an unfortunate fact of life is important; it will help to keep guilt to a minimum and reduce the incidence of 'victim-blaming' behaviour. However, given the frequency of criminal incidents today (sometimes extremely violent incidents), there is a very strong case for organizations arranging follow-up and support for members of staff who become victims. Deciding precisely what kind of help to offer must be guided and informed by an understanding of how violent incidents affect people. This will be the main theme for Chapter 6.

SUMMARY

- Preventative measures are highly organization specific.
- Where preventative measures are introduced they must be balanced against any interference with the business in other ways.
- Although many workplace incidents do not involve serious physical injury, they often involve verbal aggression, abuse and sometimes violence.
- Very few people engage in violence for the sake of violence. In most cases aggression and abuse are the result of escalating frustration over a short period of time.
- Appropriate action by an employee can often defuse many situations which otherwise would lead to aggression and violence.

6

Effects of violence and crime on individuals

INTRODUCTION

Although Chapter 3 concentrated on the effects of violence and crime on the organization, these are inextricably linked with the effects on individuals. For example, sickness absence and requests for transfers are an organizational cost but they are also the result of an individual's experience. What happens to an individual inevitably has a direct cost for the organization. They are, as it were, 'Siamese twins', who share the same event but experience its effects in different ways.

With this in mind, the focus for this chapter is the effects of violence and crime on the individual. However, in changing the focus to the individual there is again a whole spectrum of response patterns. This is equally as daunting and messy as attempting to cover all types of violence and crime which could occur at work. Indeed, the issue becomes how to make sense of the disorder and incongruity. Typically violent incidents against the person have the most lasting (and devastating) effects. However, this is not always the case, for on occasions non-violent crime can be equally debilitating. There are no simple yardsticks; so much depends on individual perceptions.

IMMEDIATE EFFECTS OF AN INCIDENT

Whereas the verbal aggression and abuse discussed in Chapter 5 generally has a 'lead time' during which preventative action can be taken, this is not the case with criminal incidents. When a crime occurs, it is usually a complete surprise for those involved. Preparation helps, but it does not take away the shock of being handed a note demanding money or looking down the barrel of a gun, perhaps coupled with obscene, demeaning language. When confronted with situations like these people generally go into a shock reaction. There may be momentary disbelief about what is happening but this nearly always quickly gives way to shock.

Shock is automatic and completely outside voluntary control. The body simply responds immediately and a complex combination of physiological, psychological and behavioural effects are set in motion. Physiologically a whole battery of chemical, hormonal and functional events take place, e.g.:

- Cortisone is released.
- Hormone levels increase, speeding up the body's metabolism.
- Endorphins are released, reducing any sensation of pain from injury.
- The digestive tract shuts down, sometimes giving a sensation of 'butterflies' in the gut. Additionally the mouth goes dry and the rectum and/or bladder may empty spontaneously (leading to real and understandable embarrassment afterwards).
- Sugar, insulin and cholesterol are released into the blood-stream.
- Heartbeat speeds up and races. Victims often describe this as 'feeling as if their heart was about to burst through their chest'.
- Nostrils flare, the throat and air passageways in the lungs dilate and breathing becomes deeper and more rapid, sometimes leading to hyperventilation and fainting/passing out.
- The blood thickens as additional blood cells are introduced into the circulation.
- The skin crawls, pales and sweats.

All in all this is quite a formidable list. However, this is not the end of the story; other perceptual, emotional and psychological effects happen at the same time, e.g.:

- All of the senses become highly acute. If the reader has ever been woken in the middle of the night through some unusual sound and thought momentarily that an intruder has been inside their house, they will have experienced this effect. It is as if all the senses suddenly becomes supersensitive to any sound or movement—hearing feels as if it is strained to catch even the slightest noise or rustle while eyes, smell and kinaesthetic senses feel stretched to the limit.

- Perceptions of time may seem to slow down. Events that take only a matter of seconds can feel like an age. Victims commonly describe incidents 'as if they were happening in slow motion'.

- Emotional responses can vary enormously. If you have never been a victim in an incident at work you might expect that the primary emotion is one of fear. Yet surveys enquiring how victims felt when confronted by an assailant indicate that a wide range of emotional reactions is quite normal. As well as fear these include:
  - feeling powerless
  - anger
  - tense
  - in control of emotions
  - feeling calm
  - feeling inadequate
  - confusion

Furthermore, it is worth noting that a significant number of victims feel at their worst a few hours *after* an incident (often when they are at home). It is equally important to remember that not everyone will be badly affected by involvement in an incident. Some people do seem to be able to take such events in their stride and quickly shrug off any adverse effects. Indeed, in instances where other colleagues are more

seriously affected, they might even start worrying that
something is 'wrong' with them for not being more affected.

- Normal thinking processes and concentration can become
confused and muddled—again victims often report 'being
unable to think straight', 'their thinking being in a tailspin' or
their brain 'going out of gear'. If company procedures require
victims to write a report of what happened as soon as possible
after the incident then even the most literate of staff can find
they are unable to write coherently.

- In a very small number of cases some victims report an 'out of
body' experience. Perhaps the easiest way to describe this
reaction is through the experience of an actual victim.

Case Study 6.1

When the raid took place I remember being terrified that he would
shoot. Then all of a sudden I felt calm and I realized that somehow I
was no longer inside my own body. Instead, I seemed to be floating
somewhere above looking down at what was happening. I know this
sounds weird but I was able to watch myself as the raider took the
money. I know I was involved, but somehow I wasn't. I felt as if I had
split in two; my body was involved in the incident, but the real me was
able to watch it take place.

Where this does occur it can be very disturbing for the individual
concerned. Afterwards they may even begin to doubt their sanity
and think their response is symptomatic of a 'breakdown' or
mental instability.

There are other psychological reactions but typically these only
start to affect victims some time after an incident has occurred.
These subsequent effects will be discussed in detail in the section
that follows. For the present we will turn our attention to the
behavioural impact of shock.

Historically the effects of shock have been described as the
'fight-flight' response. Yet, in reality 'fight-flight' is an over-
simplified and inadequate description of how people behave
when in shock. Admittedly, some people do react violently and

'have a go'; however, others may realize their predicament and, despite any internal compulsion to do otherwise, simply do as they are told and comply with an assailant's demands. Others may adopt a 'flight' response and run away and cower behind any protection they can find, but equally common (and ignored in the 'fight-flight' description) is a 'freeze' reaction, where people literally freeze, become absolutely immobile and unable to move a muscle.

The important point to emphasize is that all of the effects and reactions described in this section are perfectly normal. They are normal responses to abnormal events. However, what often surprises people is the enormous range of responses. Some people may be hardly affected whereas others may be severely traumatized. Furthermore, there is no way of predicting beforehand who will be affected and who will not. I would repeat that the very wide variation in individual need *must* be accepted as normal.

Nevertheless, although there is no way of predicting who will be affected, there do appear to be several factors that influence both the degree of shock experienced and subsequent recovery afterwards (though these are not hard and fast rules).

The severity of the incident
Incidents which are particularly brutal or exceptional often engender greater degrees of shock. Where assailants use oppressive or abusive threats, discharge firearms, physically manhandle or injure employees the degree of shock and trauma is increased. This is also the case where villains carry out a raid in an unusual or exceptional manner, as the following case illustrates.

Case Study 6.2
The raiders involved in this incident rented a vacant flat immediately above the premises they planned to raid. Once installed in the flat they removed large sections of floorboard, leaving only a thin crust of plasterboard between themselves and the office below. On the morning of the raid they waited for the brief window of time between

all of the staff arriving at work and the doors being officially opened for business. Once they were sure all of the staff were inside (and the outside doors still locked to the public) they acted. The raiders dropped through the ceiling on to the counters below wielding machetes and screaming obscenities.

One can imagine the degree of panic/terror they created. Although no one was actually injured physically, the shock and trauma experienced was immense.

Organizations frequently show their highest level of concern and care after particularly nasty incidents. Clearly this is natural and understandable. However, in large organizations where incidents are relatively common, it can lead to lower key incidents being dismissed or overlooked. It is worth remembering, therefore, that the degree of threat, violence or injury sustained in an incident is only *one* of the factors that influence how badly victims are affected. It is a major factor, but others mediate as well. It is important therefore to emphasize the following myth which is frequently either stated or inferred by armchair commentators.

'The degree of distress and trauma (and therefore time needed for recovery) which individuals experience in an incident is directly related to the level of threat/injury sustained.'

This is a widely held but very unhelpful oversimplification. For the author it was illustrated during a discussion with a manager. At the time the manager could not understand why two employees were absent from work with 'anxiety state' following their involvement in an incident. At the time of the incident the employees were locked inside the back of a stationary security vehicle. Four assailants attempted to force an entry using a sledge-hammer, pickaxes and crowbars. As the villains were unable to open the vehicle and the employees were physically unharmed (in fact they never even saw the villains), the manager could not understand why they should experience severe distress.

Suffice it to say that threat and injury are not the only factors that influence the level of shock and trauma that victims experience.

Subjective perception of trauma and the resilience/ constitution of individuals involved

We all have different perceptions of what constitutes trauma and consequently to what degree we may be affected by an incident. For some people an intimidating look coupled with being handed a scribbled note demanding money may be perceived as traumatic, whereas for others an incident is not perceived as traumatic unless it involves violent threats or physical abuse. Equally we all differ in our own personal resilience to trauma. As mentioned earlier, some people are severely affected whereas others can easily shrug off any adverse effects. What is clear is that our unique individual perceptions of an event coupled with our personal resilience/constitution does mediate in the degree to which we may be affected.

Perhaps what is also worth highlighting at this point is the need for counselling following an incident. Given the exposure and prominence that counselling has received over the past few years a new myth has started to emerge.

'Everyone who is involved in a criminal incident needs professional counselling. Furthermore, counselling is best left to the experts.'

This is simply not true. Following an incident everyone does not need counselling (let alone professional counselling). Some people need to be left alone; some need to voice their experience to a listening ear; some need advice and more extended listening and support; a few do need counselling (and sometimes professional counselling). Given adequate training and support, the vast majority of victims can be helped by peers, colleagues or friends who are prepared to devote a little time to support and listen to someone in need. The belief that counselling is needed in every case is quite simply wrong (and in a few cases is perhaps used by managers as an excuse to avoid any involvement at all).

The extent to which individuals are prepared for the possibility of an incident

Although not demonstrated conclusively, the evidence available appears to confirm that preparation and training beforehand helps to minimize the shock experienced at the time of an incident and also during subsequent recovery.

The reader may recall the case of John from Chapter 1. Although not mentioned directly, prior to the raid the belief held by the staff at John's workplace was that 'incidents are highly unlikely to happen here'. Furthermore, no preparation or training was given. The staff were aware that incidents had taken place in London and 'the South', but nothing ever happened in their locality. Hence, when John's raid did occur they were unprepared and once again it was completely unexpected. I am convinced that this complicated John's recovery. Time and time again he would repeat 'We just weren't expecting it'.

The effectiveness of social support networks

Social support networks are important aids to recovery, both at work and at home. These will be addressed more fully later, but for the present suffice it to say that where they do not exist (or do not meet a victim's needs) they can impair and prolong recovery.

The response of others who may become involved

Many other people may become involved in a victim's life. They usually include the police; sometimes doctors/hospital staff where injuries are sustained; criminal justice agencies where the villains are apprehended, charged and taken to court; perhaps even journalists or the media where an incident attracts their attention. As will be discussed later, inadvertent or thoughtless comments from any of these can (and does) complicate or inhibit recovery.

SUBSEQUENT EFFECTS OF AN INCIDENT

It is now generally accepted that exposure to traumatic/severely stressful situations can lead to emotional and behavioural disruption. This is usually described in terms of post-traumatic stress disorder (PTSD). PTSD has been widely mentioned in the press, particularly in connection with people involved with major disasters, e.g. the Kings Cross fire, the Hillsborough Football disaster, the Kegworth plane crash, the Piper Alpha disaster, etc, and the reader may have encountered the term before. It is, however, a recognized disorder which is generally diagnosed by a combination of symptoms:

- Experience of an exceptionally stressful event which could be diagnosed as the basis of the problem.
- Re-experiencing the traumatic situation. This could happen in a number of ways, e.g.:
  - recurrent intrusive and painful recollections of the event (usually called 'flashbacks')
  - repeated dreams and nightmares
  - a dissociative state lasting anywhere from a few minutes to several days where the victim acts as though they were reliving the original situation that caused the trauma, which is generally triggered by either something in the environment or by an intrusive thought (thankfully this is very rare).
- A numbing of responses to, or involvement with, the external world. This can manifest in various ways, e.g.:
  - feeling detached from all things happening in the environment
  - being unable to enjoy things which were pleasurable before the incident
  - being unable to feel close to others, feel intimacy, tenderness or sexuality.
- A variety of other symptoms, of which two must not have been present before the trauma, e.g.:
  - being hyperalert or having an exaggerated startle response

- suffering initial, middle or terminal sleep disturbance
- experiencing guilt at surviving when others perished or guilt over the actions needed in order to survive
- having memory impairment and/or trouble concentrating
- avoiding situations likely to lead to recall of the event
- suffering more intense symptoms when exposed to events, situations or activities that resemble the original trauma.
- There *may* also be depression or anxiety, occasionally in an extreme form. The victim may also become irritable and have aggressive outbursts with little or no provocation.

Note that strictly speaking **PTSD** cannot be diagnosed unless the symptoms are still present four weeks after an incident, though this is not always recognized.

The extent to which any of these symptoms impair behaviour can vary from conscious avoidance of television programmes like 'Crimewatch' through to disruption of almost every aspect of daily life. However, the previous description of **PTSD** is written in general terms and perhaps it would be of value to look specifically at how it applies to criminal incidents at work.

Experience of an exceptionally stressful event
For most people being threatened by someone with a firearm, baseball bat or knife is, by any definition, exceptionally stressful. Even 'lower key' incidents (e.g. where a potential weapon is pointed from the inside of a coat pocket) are well outside people's everyday experience. I have no hesitation in classifying any incidents of this type as exceptionally stressful.

Re-experiencing the traumatic situation
Victims of incidents at work commonly report intrusive 'flashback' memories. Often these are triggered by something which is reminiscent of a feature of the original incident, e.g.:

- A motor cyclist walking into their office or shop wearing a

crash helmet or someone wearing similar clothing to an assailant
- A child carrying a toy gun
- A man carrying an empty (or nearly empty) plastic carrier bag
- A reconstruction or report of even vaguely similar incidents on television, radio or in the press
- Equally, anniversaries can lead to re-experiencing an incident, e.g. same time or same day of the week during the early stages of recovery etc.

The list is endless. Victims also report disturbing dreams and nightmares. Sometimes these directly resemble the incident and sometimes they involve grotesque variations.

Typically both of these sets of symptoms are worst during the first few days after an incident. During the weeks that follow they generally diminish in potency. However, this is not always the case; sometimes they can extend for much longer. Indeed, if the appropriate trigger is sensitized, a victim might still experience vivid memories many years after an incident.

Numbing of responses/involvement with the outside world

Victims commonly report feeling isolated, cold, being different in some way, unable to really talk to anyone, feeling as though a thin veil (or plate of glass) has been drawn between themselves and everyone else in the world. Again, these feelings usually diminish within a few days but sometimes they persist over many months. In a minority of cases they can become a real source of difficulty, causing disruption of previously close relationships.

Other symptoms—hyperalert/startle response

Victims of criminal incidents at work frequently report being 'on edge', jumpy, easily upset following an incident. Generally this is heightened when they have to return to their normal workplace or carry out a task where the incident took place.

Sleep disturbance

All of the sleep disturbance patterns mentioned in the PTSD description are reported by victims of crime at work. Some experience no difficulty falling asleep, but then they wake up again shortly afterwards; some wake in the middle of the night; some wake two or three hours too early and cannot get back to sleep. The pattern of sleep reaction defies prediction; some people seem to be affected and some do not.

Guilt

Guilt seems to be expressed most often in two ways: firstly, by staff who were not present at the time of the incident for some reason (particularly if whoever took their place was a central figure in the incident) and, secondly, by managers or supervisors who may (or may not) have been present at the time of the incident and feel they 'should have done more' to protect their staff.

Memory impairment/difficulty concentrating

Following an incident victims commonly find difficulty concentrating on what were previously everyday routines (both at work and at home). Equally a few report becoming more forgetful. It is also worth highlighting the fact that very often the effects of an incident are most evident at home. It is as if victims make a special effort to cope at work but 'let go' when at home.

Avoidance behaviour

Many victims experience a natural reluctance to return to the place where the incident occurred—often their normal place at work. However, unlike crime elsewhere, at work avoidance is generally not an option: the bank or building society cashier has to return to dealing with the public; the security guard has to go back to collection and delivery duties; the shop assistant has to go back to working the till. For all of them refusal to return to their normal work would probably mean they could no longer be employed. Nowadays few organizations have 'other duties' where staff could be employed, even temporarily. Even where such employment does exist, sooner or later staff must return to their normal work station. Although most victims manage this, some do not. Sadly, for them the only options are resignation or ill-health retirement.

Intensification of symptoms
The avoidance behaviours described in the previous section are usually a direct result of anxiety over intensification of symptoms. Victims generally feel much worse when they first return to the scene where the incident took place. However, these are not the only triggers which lead to deterioration. Anything which reminds the victim often leads to a similar outcome. In particular it is worth mentioning involvement in police investigations and/or judicial processes; these will be discussed more fully later.

Depression/anxiety
Depression and/or anxiety often follows involvement in an incident. As with many of the other symptoms this is usually relatively brief and passes quite quickly, but on some occasions it may become more prolonged and require medical intervention.

COMING TO TERMS WITH AN INCIDENT

Although the medical definition of PTSD is important, if nothing else, it has helped to give formal recognition to the fact that involvement with traumatic incidents can be extremely disturbing. However, it does not aid our understanding of how victims come to terms with such events. For this we must look elsewhere.

During my own work with victims I have found the general model of how people come to terms with major life crises/ incidents very useful. Before addressing this in any detail I would like to invite the reader to complete the following exercise. It should help illuminate some of the processes described by the model.

Exercise 6.1

On a blank sheet of paper make a list of two or three major incidents or events that have happened in your life. If you have been a victim of a criminal incident at some time, then include this on your list. If not you could use experiences like:

- *Bereavement of a close family member*
- *Involvement in a serious road traffic accident*
- *Significant personal loss*
- *Compulsory redundancy*
- *etc.*

Should you find yourself in the position of never having experienced a major incident then try to think of someone you know well who has been through such an experience.

When your list is complete, for each event make a few notes on:

- *How you/they felt while coming to terms with the incident/event.*
- *How you/they behaved during the process.*
- *What helped you/them cope.*
- *How you/they felt after having come to terms with the incident/ event.*

Finally keep these notes close to hand as you read the rest of this section.

The general model of how people come to terms with major life incidents/events typically involves six stages, these are:

- Shock
- Denial/minimization
- Depression
- Acceptance/letting go
- Reconstruction/rehabilitation
- Normalization

In order to illustrate how this model applies to workplace incidents each of these stages will be considered in turn.

Shock
As we saw earlier, a victim's initial reaction is usually shock. This

has already been examined in considerable detail and therefore will not be discussed further here.

Denial/minimization

Once the immediate shock effects have diminished they are commonly replaced by a period of denial or minimization. During this time the full impact of what has happened starts to take effect—the level of threat to which the victim was exposed, perhaps also what could have happened if things had gone differently. However, although all of these thoughts may be whirling round in a victim's mind their behaviour is often to minimize or make light of their experience. Sometimes they could even deny that it is bothering them at all (despite the fact that they may be unable to think of little else).

Although denial/minimization is a normal stage which victims go through, it does lead to difficulty in discriminating between people who are genuinely minimally affected by an incident and those who are starting to suffer quite badly but maintaining a façade of feeling fine. This can lead to additional difficulties for anyone involved in helping victims and this will be addressed more fully in Chapter 8.

Depression

Denial and minimization can give way to depression as victims struggle to make sense of their experience. As mentioned earlier, usually this is short lived and passes quite quickly. However, in a small number of cases purely normal reactive depression becomes deeper and more serious and will require medical intervention.

Furthermore, without being overdramatic, it must also be pointed out that sometimes a few victims become so depressed they start to feel that life is no longer worth living. Only rarely will they actually use the word suicide themselves; more often they use expressions like 'not wanting to go on', 'wishing it would all end', 'feeling there is no point any more'. Phrases such as these *must* be taken very seriously. In themselves they do not necessarily mean that a victim is thinking about suicide, but in some cases they do. In addition, before closing this section, one very important common myth must be mentioned.

'People who talk about suicide are not serious. If they were serious they would simply go out and do it.'

This is absolutely wrong. The vast majority of people (around 95 per cent or more) who successfully terminate their own lives give warning beforehand. Very, very few take their own lives without giving some kind of warning in what they say or do—more often these warnings are either not heard, dismissed as not being serious or are ignored by people who hear them.

Any victim who talks about 'not wanting to go on', 'wishing the lights could be turned out', 'not wanting to face another day', etc., *must* be taken seriously and if necessary offered more professional help.

Acceptance/letting go

The early stages of coming to terms with major incidents/events are often characterized by retrospective thinking, where victims long for everything to be as it was before the incident took place. For example, sometimes they use expressions like 'wishing it had never happened and the clock could be turned back' or 'wishing they had chosen to have the day off'. In many respects they cannot make progress until they accept that what has happened has happened and history cannot be rewritten (much though they would wish otherwise). Eventually they will (usually) return to normal, but it will not be the same normality as before the incident. This crucial stage in recovery concerns victims accepting fully the reality of what has happened and letting go of life as it was.

Sometimes victims are able to negotiate this stage very quickly; some describe it being like a switch being turned inside their heads, bringing with it the realization that they are ready to move forwards once again. In other cases the process takes longer and is more fragmented, as if acceptance can only be carried out a little at a time.

Reconstruction/rehabilitation

The penultimate stage of recovery is where victims start to rebuild their lives and look forward to the future with some degree of optimism. Nevertheless, they would be the first to accept that this is very different to the way they thought prior to the incident.

It is also important to recognize that reconstruction is rarely a smooth process. Generally it is characterized by 'ups and downs'. On some days victims will feel they have made real progress but on others they may feel as bad as ever. As one victim described it, 'It's a bit like trying to climb up a sand dune—even though you try to climb upwards you keep on slipping back again.'

Normalization

Reconstruction finally gives way to a new normality. In this final stage the memories of the incident recede into the background and no longer intrude as they did earlier. The incident is never completely forgotten but it no longer intrudes into everyday life. One victim described her memories as 'being just out of reach'. However, even after a full recovery (and this is not always the case) if the appropriate trigger is squeezed the images flood back as vivid and detailed as ever.

Although I find this description useful in aiding my own understanding of recovery, it must be approached with caution. As with most behavioural models it should be seen as flexible. The boundaries between each of the stages are never clear cut; they are more a general guide than concrete categorical descriptions. Equally progress through each of the stages does not necessarily follow a smooth sequence; at times victims might oscillate between stages.

No doubt you will also have noted that I have given no

indication of how long the process might take. This is because it is so extremely variable and, as will be highlighted in the section which follows, so many other factors can introduce additional complications. Equally the model gives no indication of the extent to which people may be affected at each stage. Once again, this is similarly highly variable. At one extreme some people shrug off any effects without any noticeable effect on their behaviour, whereas at the other extreme a few become 'stuck' in the depression stage and never recover.

COMPLICATING FACTORS

In common with other types of crime, criminal incidents at work are sometimes plagued by a host of complications.

Family reactions

In order to try and gauge your own reaction to incidents at work, try to complete the following exercise before you read any further.

Exercise 6.2
Imagine you are at home and a close member of your household (e.g. partner, spouse, son or daughter) is late home from work. Eventually they arrive about half an hour late looking very distressed and accompanied by a colleague from where they work. You discover they have been involved in an armed raid at work. Two villains screaming abuse had stormed the office/shop where he/she works. He/she was at the centre and was threatened aggressively by one of the villains with a sawn-off shotgun. They are absolutely convinced that if someone had put a foot wrong they would have been shot.
Close your eyes and try to imagine this scene happening in your home as vividly as you can. Make a note of your reactions/how you feel. Finally, try to compare your response with the text that follows.

Although this is a gross oversimplification (and perhaps very unfair in many individual instances), very often the immediate reaction when a partner or spouse has been involved in an incident is initially concern—e.g. 'is she alright?', 'what happened?'. However, this is commonly rapidly followed by anger—e.g. 'how could they have put her in such a position?', 'why didn't they do something?' (sometimes these reactions are the other way round; anger comes first and is only followed by concern if the victim becomes upset).

Sadly, although understandable, other people's anger is probably the last emotion that a victim needs to feel in the hours following an incident (particularly from their partner or spouse). It only serves to feed their sense of isolation and prevents them talking through their experience in relationships where they should feel supported.

By contrast a more helpful reaction is to be supportive from the outset. Other family members can also play a role in providing support, though once again (in the absence of training) this is not necessarily the case.

Financial difficulties

Usually the people who are most at risk from criminal violence or threat are those in the lower pay/salary bands of an organization. Quite often their basic pay is supplemented (sometimes quite extensively) by overtime, bonus or some other form of premium payment. Furthermore, where staff have come to expect overtime or bonus to boost their basic rate, then typically their lifestyle will reflect the higher income level. Therefore, where a company is not prepared to grant average earnings to staff who are absent following an incident, then those who are seriously affected (and, as a consequence, need extended sick leave) could also face financial difficulty. For them this will appear to add insult to injury. They will feel that they have become victims twice over; once as a result of criminal action and again through organizational insensitivity.

Comments by insensitive customers

The reader may find it difficult to believe but comments or actions by customers can be the most cutting of all. These are best illustrated through two brief case studies. The first is relatively common, the second much rarer, but taken together they do illustrate the range of unhelpful ways in which customers can react.

Case Study 6.3

A small building society branch had been raided two days earlier. The cashier involved had been threatened by a man with a hand-gun and had filled a plastic bag with a few hundred pounds in bank notes. The raider left and no one was injured. However, the raid was reported by the local radio and in the local press.

The cashier did not take any time off and reported for work the following day; this passed without incident. On the second day, still feeling guilty about giving away the money, she was approached by an elderly lady (who had been a customer with the branch for many years). After making light conversation for a few moments the lady said, 'I hear you were robbed earlier this week.' The cashier agreed and the lady responded with, 'Well I hope you didn't given them any of my money.'

For the cashier this was too much; she screamed and ran off into the back office in tears. Only timely intervention by the manager stopped the lady making alternative financial arrangements elsewhere.

Case Study 6.4

On the day following a robbery a male customer entered the building society branch where the raid had taken place. On entering he pulled his overcoat collar up around his face, approached the counter, made his fist into a gun shape, pointed it at a cashier and commented (in a Jimmy Cagney type voice), 'You gave them the money, now give me some.'

The staff at the counter had been involved in the raid on the day before and were still feeling the effects. Their response can be left to the reader's imagination.

The vast majority of unhelpful customer comments are the result of ignorance. Customers simply do not know what it is like to be involved in an incident at work. Their intention, very often, is well meaning. However, for victims their comments and actions can create unwelcome additional difficulties. Accepting that most customer comments are well intended, I sometimes wonder whether the remaining few are motivated by more devious, perhaps even malicious, intent.

Insensitive managers

Most managers are intensely concerned when any of their staff have been involved in an incident. Some 'pull out all the stops' to ensure that they have as much help as possible. However, unfortunately there are a few others who are much less sympathetic and expect staff to get back to normal in unrealistically short time-scales. Typically they have little tolerance for any avoidance behaviour on the part of victims. Even where concessions are granted, they are granted begrudgingly.

As mentioned earlier, avoidance is a common reaction following any crime. Helping staff gently ease back into their normal role (assuming this was where the incident occurred) is generally very helpful. Conversely, the level of stress which staff experience may become intolerable if they are pushed (or bullied) into carrying out tasks for which they feel unprepared. As a consequence they are likely to make more mistakes, become forgetful or accident prone, and generally become either less communicative/short tempered or moody. This, in turn, may be interpreted by an unsympathetic manager as evidence that they are no longer coping (i.e. not 'up to the job') and reflect in subsequent appraisals. For the victim this could mark the start of a downward spiral.

Alternatively, where victims feel trapped in their current employment, they may do their best to cope at work. Instead, the pressure they feel they are under manifests in problems at home.

Coincidental Events

For victims other things sometimes go wrong or happen coincidentally around the same time as an incident at work. In many respects this seems like an illustration of the old adage 'trouble comes in threes'. I have seen this phenomenon occur time and time again—once one thing happens, several others occur in quick succession. Take, for example, John whose case was described in Chapter 1. In the months which followed his incident he seemed to be followed by a trail of disaster; practically everything that could go wrong did, for example he was unfairly assessed as only 10 per cent disabled, his house was burgled, renewal of his car insurance was refused, etc. One could argue that this was all simply coincidence, yet coincidence does seem to happen to some victims with monotonous regularity. The following case study gives another illustration.

Case Study 6.5

Tim had been absent from work for about 10 weeks following a particularly brutal assault. Although fully recovered from his physical injuries he was still very anxious about returning to his old job (as a delivery driver). The organization had therefore agreed he could ease his way back in by working reduced hours for the first few weeks.

However, on his first day back, together with a colleague, he was asked to deliver some correspondence to a local office. They took a company van and the colleague chose to drive, while Tim sat in the passenger seat. As they left the delivery bay Tim's colleague suffered a major heart attack and was rushed off to hospital. Although there was no way that Tim could have been responsible for this coincidence, it did not aid his re-entry back to work.

Although some of the things which go wrong in a victim's life following an incident are directly connected with the incident, I continue to be amazed at how many are not (even the most unexpected of events). Clearly, complications such as these are not helpful from a victim's point of view. However, it is important for anyone who is involved with supporting victims to recognize and acknowledge that such complications do happen (sometimes creating additional problems for recovery).

Newspaper and media involvement

In some respects newspaper and media involvement following an incident can be a mixed blessing. On the one hand some victims are willing and want to talk to the press. Indeed, they sometimes find the interviews helpful as a means of expressing their experience and are upset if 'their' incident is not reported. However, there are other cases where the methods used to obtain a 'story' are highly intrusive. Press photographers and telephoto lenses can be a nightmare. Furthermore, what is said during a press interview may be reported in a completely different manner or context. Where victims are interviewed by the press, they are sometimes devastated by what they read subsequently. Phrases and quotes can be taken out of context, juxtaposed against other views or generally messed around. In the eyes of the press this is all quite legitimate. However, for a victim the result can be horrifying. They may feel exposed, vulnerable and let down by interviewers they assumed they could trust.

Yet press and media interest does tend to be a one-day wonder. What is news today is generally history tomorrow. Press and media concern usually fades very rapidly. Victims who were the centre of attention one day may be forgotten on the next. This can in turn exacerbate their sense of isolation and loss. This is most apparent where the press find a 'hero'—usually someone who 'had a go', 'risked their life' or perhaps 'saved the day'. But yet again, even heroes become history when another 'story' unfolds.

In large companies where the press and media are concerned it may be company policy that any communication is carried out through the public relations department. However, where this is not the case it is perhaps best if victims are allowed a choice about whether they speak to the press or not. Furthermore, from a press and media point of view I would urge them to respect the wishes of victims and to treat both victims and their stories with tact and sensitivity. Finally, where either victims or organizations believe they have been treated unfairly or misrepresented then it is worth remembering that complaints may be lodged through the Press Complaints Commission.

Involvement in police investigatory procedures

By virtue that a crime has taken place, victims will usually become involved with police inquiries. Initially this will mean talking through with an officer what happened and then making a formal statement. Usually this whole procedure will take place at the victim's workplace or at a local police station (on rare occasions statements may be taken at the victim's home). Over the last few years the police have become much more aware of, and sensitive to, victims' needs. Typically their interviews are thorough but carried out in a tactful and sensitive manner. On the whole victims report that police behaviour immediately following an incident is both supportive and reassuring.

The degree of involvement which victims have with the police beyond this point very much depends on the progress of the investigation, in particular, whether any suspect is taken in and held for questioning (or charged with the crime). Where this does happen victims may be asked to help by identifying the suspect in an identity parade.

Many people expect identity parades to take place from behind the security of a one-way mirror. Generally they are horrified when it does not. Very few police stations in this country are equipped with one-way mirrors. Assisting with an identity parade means that the victim will have to walk down a line of people only a few feet away and choose which one they believe carried out the crime. Most find this experience very disturbing. Typically it re-awakens their memories about the incident and can trigger a shock reaction similar to the one they experienced when the incident took place. Although the police are generally supportive and recognize the effect of this procedure, for victims it can cause regression rather than recovery.

Before leaving this section it is important to point out that I am *not* suggesting that victims should refuse to help with identity parades. Their evidence is sometimes crucial in obtaining a conviction. However, we do need to recognize and acknowledge the effects of identity parades and, as will be suggested later, additional support can be very helpful. Where this is not possible internally within an organization through colleagues or other members of staff, it may be possible to arrange external help through organizations like Victim Support.

Giving evidence in court

Only a small proportion of criminal incidents at work ever reach court. Where they do, both victims and others who witnessed the incident may be called to give evidence. This experience can be at best confusing and intimidating; at worst, devastating, so much so that the national organization Victim Support has initiated a widespread Witness Service in the Crown Courts (this is mentioned further in Appendix 1 for any reader who is interested).

When a victim appears in court as a witness it will probably be the first time they have set foot inside a courtroom. They will be unused to the language and customs and practice of court procedures. This can be very intimidating. Their first glimpse of the accused may also come as a surprise. If the accused who attacked them was scruffy and unkempt, the man standing in the dock may seem very presentable by comparison, perhaps even clean shaven and wearing a suit. His family will probably seem very close by, perhaps his wife and parents, and perhaps also any brothers and sisters. By now even the most confident of witnesses will be starting to wilt.

After taking the oath, the questioning will begin. Usually the victim will be a witness for the prosecution and generally questions from the prosecution will be relatively straightforward. The difficulties start if the defence counsel choose to cross-examine. The judicial systems in the UK are adversarial by design. In effect this means that each side (both prosecution and defence) has an opportunity to present its own case and test the reliability and robustness of the case presented by the other.

The victim may therefore be questioned by the defence in microscopic detail about what happened. Given that by now many months will have elapsed since the incident took place, the effect of this type of questioning can be harrowing. Victims commonly leave the witness stand feeling utter failures; many have said they felt as if they were criminals themselves. Victims who have appeared in court often describe their experience as demeaning, humiliating, harrowing or unfair. There are even a small number who, as a result of their experience, are resolved that if they ever become involved in another incident they will maintain from the outset that they saw nothing.

As an author and practitioner who has tried to help many victims come to terms with their experience, I obviously have my own personal view on this whole process. However, for the present perhaps it is best if I keep my own counsel. Suffice it to say that giving evidence in court can trigger significant deterioration in a victim's recovery. Indeed, deterioration often starts at the point when they hear that the case is going to court or they receive notification (or a summons) to attend court. Anxiety increases, vivid memories return and many of the symptoms described earlier may once again become features in the victim's life. Even after they have given evidence, the subsequent effects can be quite alarming.

Case Study 6.6

Mary was called to give evidence (along with two of her colleagues) about an armed raid which took place in their shop several months earlier. She was called to the witness stand fairly early during the prosecution case. After the prosecution barrister had established what Mary thought were the facts, the defence counsel chose to cross-examine. She felt his questioning was relentless and interrogatory. She became confused and upset and eventually was thankful to be released from her ordeal. Although her colleagues pleaded with her to remain to see the outcome of the trial, Mary felt she could not re-enter the court. Instead, in a confused state of mind, she returned to work.

On entering the shop Mary felt a sense of panic. It was as if all of her experiences of the raid and the courtroom were happening once again inside her mind. Her rate of breathing increased, she hyperventilated, passed out and collapsed on the floor.

Mary's manager was frantic. Quite naturally he called an ambulance and Mary was taken to the local hospital where, over the next few hours, she slowly calmed down and was eventually allowed home. Ironically, although Mary had not been absent from work following the raid itself, her experience on giving evidence led to several days' absence.

One further aspect of the judicial process concerns the effect of sentencing. Where villains are apprehended, charged, tried and found guilty, the effect of the sentence passed can also have a tremendous impact on victims. Where victims feel the sentence is appropriate it is usually greeted with relief, as if their ordeal has been worth the effort. However, in cases where the sentence seems inappropriate victims feel let down and disappointed, as if all they have been through had been a waste of time and effort.

In conclusion, I would simply like to emphasize once again that, for victims, involvement in the court process is always stressful. I believe that appropriate support and understanding at this stage is essential. Where this cannot be arranged internally within a company, the Victim Support Witness Service may be able to help.

The effects of DSS Medical Reviews

In cases where employees are absent from work for several months (or more), at some stage they will be required to attend a DSS Medical Review. Unless a victim has been permanently physically disabled during the incident, by this stage any physical injury will probably have healed. The reason for their absence will more than likely be psychological, typically severe post-traumatic stress disorder.

Although only few in number, these cases are particularly

distressing. They are people whose lives have been ruined by what should have been a normal day at work. With respect to medical reviews, unless the doctor conducting the review demonstrates extreme sensitivity the victim is unlikely to be able to give a coherent report about their condition. The review will trigger flashback memories together with all of the symptoms of shock which they experienced when the incident first occurred. At the end of the review they are likely to feel 'back at square one', as they did in the days and weeks immediately following the incident.

I recognize the need for such reviews but would advise extreme sensitivity where victims trying to recover from PTSD are concerned.

Criminal Injuries Compensation

Although well intended, for a few victims Criminal Injuries Compensation can become a final hurdle. Generally Criminal Injury Compensation claims take years before any conclusion is reached. In the meantime severely affected victims may feel unable finally to come to terms with their experience. It is as if the whole experience is a massive jigsaw puzzle and Criminal Injuries Compensation is the final piece. Their experience cannot be laid to rest until the puzzle is complete. Recently there has been considerable concern over the length of time taken by Criminal Injuries Compensation. I can only add my own voice to calls for the process to be speeded up.

Multiple events

With incidents at work complications through multiple events generally manifest in one of two ways:

1. Firstly, with individuals who work in premises that are subject to violent incidents on a relatively frequent basis (e.g. some premises have been subject to incidents 10 or more times in the space of two years). The people involved in these multiple

incidents are often demoralized and constantly 'on edge', wondering when the next incident will occur. Unless an incident is exceptional, the features of each individual event can blur into one amorphous mass. On other occasions, victims may appear to recover from their first experience quite easily and show no adverse effects. However, involvement in subsequent incidents (even though they may be very low-key by comparison with the first) may generate an overwhelming reaction. In the eyes of those not involved the reaction can seem totally out of proportion. However, for the victim it is as if subsequent incidents trigger a latent reaction from the first. It underlines even further their sense of vulnerability.

Despite any concern within the organization at Area or Head Office level, the employees involved commonly feel the organization does not 'give a damn' about their situation. Furthermore, unless action is taken which either removes the possibility of further incidents or provides adequate protection for staff then the outcome will be a downward spiral and even further demoralization (perhaps leading to higher levels of absence or staff turnover, which could have been avoided).

2. Individuals who are already coping with one major life incident (e.g. bereavement, separation or divorce, etc.) when they also become involved in an incident at work. Multiple events of this type are in many ways yet another illustration of 'coincidental events' in action. Sometimes people are trying to cope/come to terms with other major events in their life when they also find themselves involved in an incident at work. Although totally unconnected, their response to one may fuel and exacerbate their reaction to the other. These cases are often more complex and could prove to be beyond the skills of ordinary support networks within an organization. Unless the company employs a more professional counsellor, it may be necessary to draw on external help.

Overall the main effect of all of these complicating factors is that they drag out and extend the time taken for victims to recover from their experience. Very often others who have not been through such an experience find it difficult to understand and, as a consequence, lose patience within a few weeks. This is graphically illustrated by an expression used by one victim who was trying hard to come to terms with both a bereavement and involvement in a violent incident—in her words, 'It's as if I've gone past my "grieve by" date.'

GROUPS THAT MAY NEED SPECIAL ATTENTION

Although we saw earlier that there is no way of predicting beforehand who will be affected by an incident, there are a few groups of people who, for a variety of reasons, may need particular attention. This does not mean they will necessarily be adversely affected, but they may have particular needs which need to be addressed.

People who may be adversely affected by shock
Involvement in an incident generally evokes a shock reaction. Heart rate accelerates, blood pressure increases and, as we have seen earlier, a whole host of chemical and hormonal changes take place within the body. All of these effects can become a source of concern for anyone suffering from a medical or psychological condition which could be aggravated by sudden shock (e.g. heart and cardio-vascular disorders). Similarly, women who are pregnant at the time of an incident may be equally concerned.

Without being alarmist, as a safety measure I would suggest that anyone who is concerned about their health and is involved in an incident visits their GP for a check-up as soon as reasonably possible. Clearly this suggestion *must* be broached very tactfully; it is important not to increase the anxiety levels of victims even further. Nevertheless, I believe that to act otherwise is simply a risk not worth taking. It is also a small gesture which demonstrates organizational concern. However, one of the difficulties in carrying out the suggestion is that some people choose not to disclose their condition unless they are forced. This presents an organizational dilemma. A company may genuinely wish to help staff, but it cannot and should not pry into personal or medical affairs. There is no procedure or policy that could be adopted to overcome this. All that can be re-emphasized is that anyone directly concerned with helping victims should behave with a high degree of sensitivity and tact and, if necessary *gently* encourage them to visit their G.P.

Very young members of staff

Very young members of staff (e.g. those working part-time after school or on a weekend, or those in their first job) may be profoundly influenced by an incident. Furthermore, unless they are approached with extreme sensitivity and understanding on the part of any supporter, they may be unwilling or unable to talk about their experience.

People who live alone

Following involvement in an incident at work people who live alone can experience particularly distressing after-effects which sometimes lead to disturbing behaviour patterns outside work.

Case Study 6.7

Sally had been involved in an incident at work about a week earlier. Although she did not take any time off, throughout the week which followed she felt increasingly insecure at home. Sally had divorced her husband some six months earlier and as a consequence lived alone.

Following the raid she found that on entering her house on an evening she had to go through each room systematically slamming open all the doors to make sure no one was inside. While at home she felt constantly on edge and uneasy. However, night-time and the hours of darkness were the worst. The only way that Sally found she could sleep was by leaving every light in the house switched on throughout the night.

It was as if the absence of social/emotional support at home conspired to make Sally's experience even worse.

It is also worth noting that similar behavioural effects can sometimes manifest with people whose spouse (or partner) works unsocial hours (e.g. nights) or who works away from home for extended periods. Very often the only time they feel safe is when their spouse/partner is around. Furthermore, if this type of behaviour continues for any length of time it can become a source of strain within the relationship.

Managers who are involved

In some organizations managers who are involved in an incident can find themselves in an invidious position. On the one hand they may need support and help themselves as a result of their own personal experience, yet at the same time there may be a strong organizational expectation that they will be the provider of support and help for other staff who were involved. The dilemma for managers in this position is crystallized in the following quotation: as one manager put it, 'How can I provide help for others when really I need help myself? Who looks after my needs?'

In very formal (or highly competitive) organizations this difficulty may be exacerbated even further. If the organizational culture is one where asking for help is perceived as a sign of weakness (or, in some cases, failure) then managers in particular will be under immense pressure to hide how they really feel. They will fear that even a hint that something could be wrong will reflect in any future performance review or appraisal. As a result they may become even more stressed as time goes by. Although one could argue that this complication could affect all staff, it is particularly relevant for managerial groups by virtue of their position and status (and the possible effects on their future career progression).

This is an issue which only an organization can do something about. Although it sounds trite, victims are victims, and if an organization's culture adds additional complications to their recovery then the culture really ought to change. Where staff are subject to abuse and violence from external sources then further internal abuse merely adds insult to injury.

EFFECTS ON BYSTANDERS

As was mentioned in Chapter 2, violent incidents and trauma can affect not only those who were directly involved, but also others who either:

- Witnessed the event or
- Should have been involved but for some reason were absent at the time the incident took place.

Although there are sometimes similarities in how these two groups react, there are also significant differences. The text which follows will therefore discuss each of them separately.

Witnesses to incidents

In some circumstances witnesses to incidents can be subject to a similar range of reactions as victims themselves, dependent on their knowledge/perception of the incident. At one extreme they may be completely oblivious that a 'low-key' raid is taking place, perhaps even with the person working next to them and maybe no more than an arm's length away (e.g. where a threatening note is passed silently to a cashier or sales assistant, perhaps backed up with a concealed weapon).

For the witness the incident only becomes a reality after the villain has left the premises. In the aftermath and over the next few days (weeks?) they may find themselves feeling guilty, going over what they remember in their mind time and time again. Commonly their anxieties circulate around questions like 'What could I have done?—I didn't even know what was happening?', 'If only I had ...'. In part their reactions may also depend on the extent to which the direct victim is affected. For example, if the victim is largely unaffected, witnesses might also be able to recover very quickly; conversely, where victims are badly affected then witnesses might well feel proportionately more guilty.

At the other extreme witnesses may be present during very noisy, abusive or violent incidents. Although in reality they might not have been directly involved themselves, they could well feel as if they were. Consequently their reactions may be little different from victims themselves. Indeed, in very nasty incidents the distinction between victim and witness is somewhat academic; to all intents and purposes they are victims as well, as the following case study illustrates.

Case Study 6.8

Maureen was working quite close to the staff rest room door when two attackers raided the shop where she worked. Maureen saw what was happening, panicked and, unseen by the attackers, dashed into the rest room frantically calling for help. Two security guards were taking a coffee break and, on seeing the state Maureen was in, one of them ran out into the shop. The villains, taken by surprise, spun round to face the guard. Without any further verbal exchange one of them fired a shotgun and the pair made their escape. The security guard fell to the floor having sustained serious injuries to his lower body and legs. When Maureen heard the gunshot she ran out from the rest room and stayed with the guard until an ambulance arrived.

Over the weeks and months which followed Maureen examined and re-examined her actions time and time again. Although not physically injured herself, and in many ways 'on the sidelines', she was as much a victim as the guard. In her imagination she saw herself as the cause of his injuries. Logically one could argue that it was not her fault, that she did not pull the trigger, but in her mind she might as well have done.

Thankfully incidents with this degree of violence are relatively infrequent. However, they do serve to underline the point that witnesses may be quite badly affected as well and should not be ignored.

Unfortunately, as was highlighted in Chapter 2, accepting responsibility for helping witnesses (and sometimes victims) is not necessarily straightforward. By virtue that most incidents take place in public settings, as we have seen earlier, sometimes customers and/or members of the general public are involved. Where this is the case, other considerations will need to be taken into account.

Staff who are absent at the time an incident takes place

Staff may be absent from work for a variety of reasons, holidays, illness or perhaps even just out at lunch. Understanding how and why they may be affected by an incident when they were not even present can be a little more difficult to understand.

Nevertheless, it does sometimes happen. Obviously this is not always the case; some people feel sheer relief that they were not involved. However, for others their absence can lead to guilt and anxiety because they feel they 'should' have been there, particularly if the colleague who took their place was severely affected or injured in the incident.

Furthermore, when the absentee returns to work they are likely to feel alone, isolated and no longer a member of the team. A significant (perhaps even major) event has happened to the group which they did not share. As a consequence they will feel that they are different in some way and in some instances blamed by the rest.

Finally, it is important to point out that absentees are easily overlooked in any initiative to provide help for staff. This commonly happens with part-time staff, temporary staff and staff who may be on loan or short-term transfer from another office.

SUMMARY

• Both during an incident and immediately afterwards, victims experience a complex, automatic shock reaction; this affects them physiologically, psychologically, emotionally and behaviourally.

- The degree of shock experienced may be affected by:
  - the severity of the incident
  - an individual's subjective perception of trauma coupled with their own personal resilience/constitution
  - the extent to which victims were prepared for the possibility of an incident
  - the effectiveness of social support networks both at work and at home
  - the response of others who may become involved
- The subsequent effects of involvement in an incident have generally been described in terms of post-traumatic stress disorder. This involves a suite of diagnostic symptoms, e.g.:
  - intrusive flashback memories of the event
  - numbing of responses
  - assuming they were not present before the incident, any two or more of being hyperalert or exhibiting an exaggerated startle response; sleep disturbance; guilt; memory impairment; difficulty concentrating; avoidance behaviour
  - intensification of symptoms when reminded of the incident
  - depression/anxiety
- The recovery pattern which victims often go through following post-traumatic stress has six phases: shock, denial/minimization, depression, acceptance/letting go, reconstruction/rehabilitation and finally normalization
- Recovery can be complicated by a whole host of factors, e.g.:
  - family reactions
  - financial difficulties
  - comments by insensitive customers (or managers)
  - coincidental events and/or multiple incidents
  - newspaper and media involvement
  - police investigatory and judicial procedures
  - DSS medical reviews
  - Criminal Injuries Compensation claims
- Some groups at work may need special attention, e.g.:

- people who may be adversely affected by shock
- very young members of staff
- people who live alone
- managers who may have been involved
- Incidents at work can affect not only those who were directly involved but also others who witnessed the event, as well as, sometimes, staff who would normally have been present but for some reason were absent when the incident took place.

7

Responding effectively

WHAT KIND OF RESPONSE IS HELPFUL?

The first half of this book has looked in some detail at violence and crime at work: the size of the problem and its effects on both the organization and members of staff. Hopefully, by now the case for taking action is firmly established. However, as the main types of incidents considered here are initiated by people outside of the organization, there is a limit to how far incidents can be prevented. Therefore, if incidents cannot be stopped altogether, it is sensible to ask what response can be made to minimize any effects. This is the major theme for the chapters that follow. Our starting point is to ask what kind of response is effective.

Because of the frequency of violence and crime some organizations are now starting to respond in a variety of ways. Clearly the type of response should be driven by the types of incidents that take place (hence the importance of a monitoring system to ensure any organizational action is appropriate). As we have seen, the range of incidents that take place is very wide; at one extreme they include crimes against property where no one is involved at the time of the incident (e.g. burglary), the bulk of incidents which involve verbal aggression, abuse and sometimes violence, through to the other extreme which involves extreme violence. Nevertheless, despite the wide variety, responding effectively can involve a number of approaches:

- Designing and implementing appropriate organizational procedures so that staff know what to do in the event of an incident

- Staff training and re-training at regular intervals
- Implementing procedure reviews following any incident
- Helping staff develop personal coping strategies that minimize the psychological impact of an incident
- Where necessary, providing follow-up and support for staff who have been involved in incidents

Before considering each of these approaches in any detail it is worth pointing out once again that although assault, robbery and high-profile incidents usually generate most concern, it must also be accepted that they are generally the tip of the iceberg. Incidents involving solely abuse and aggression are typically far more commonplace. Furthermore, they can leave the staff badly shaken and unable to carry out their normal duties for a couple of hours or more. The following case study gives a graphic illustration.

Case Study 7.1

Anna worked as a sales assistant in a high street retail outlet of a large clothing company. One morning she was approached by a customer demanding her money back on some items of clothing she had bought two weeks earlier during the summer sale. As the value of the items was above £25.00, company policy dictated that Sally examined both the clothing and the customer's receipt prior to agreeing to any refund. Unfortunately the customer interpreted this as prevarication and immediately flew into a rage, practically spitting out personal abuse and offensive swear words directly at Anna. Anna panicked, fearing the customer would become violent. However, thankfully the store manager took over and ushered the customer into a more private office. In the meantime Anna retreated to the rest room, visibly shaking from the encounter. It took the rest of the morning for her to calm down sufficiently for her to resume her normal work.

APPROPRIATE ORGANIZATIONAL PROCEDURES

Above all, staff need to know what to do in the event of an incident; pretending the problem does not exist will no longer suffice. Employees need to know precisely what to do when confronted by an aggressor. In simple terms this means having a procedure (or guidelines) which they can follow automatically.

As far as staff are concerned the main purpose of any procedure should be threefold. It should seek to:

1. Minimize the degree of risk to individual employees.
2. Provide some measure of psychological security (in that they know what to do).
3. In the case of robbery, it should also seek to minimize any goods or money stolen, though this should never compromise personal safety.

Additionally, the very existence of a procedure (particularly if it is rehearsed on a regular basis) actively demonstrates recognition by the organization that incidents happen, and concern to ensure that employees do not suffer any harm. However, BIFU point out that the development of procedure is sometimes carried out in haste.[9] Rushing through a procedure is sometimes a form of organizational 'knee-jerk' following a particularly nasty incident. To be effective it is essential that any procedure is developed from the results of internal research (such as the survey and monitoring techniques described in Chapter 4). If not, there is a fair chance that the procedure will be seen as irrelevant by the staff who have to implement it.

Obviously the detail of any procedure will vary from one organization to another and from one type of incident to another. For example, the procedure used in a bank or building society will be very different to that required by a security or haulage company; similarly, recommendations on how staff should behave when confronted by an angry or aggressive customer will be different to how they should behave when confronted by an armed robber. Nevertheless, there are key features which any procedure should consider. These include:

• The general approach to be adopted by staff (e.g. usually with more serious incidents) is to offer no resistance and never endanger either themselves or anyone else.

- The policy regarding handing over of money or goods.
- The procedure to be adopted immediately after an incident, e.g.:
  - What to do if anyone is injured.
  - Who to inform—Head Office, the police, security, next of kin of all those involved. (There have been several cases where partners found out about an incident through reports on local radio. It can be left to the reader's imagination to construct how they subsequently felt about the company involved.)
  - What to say in response to any press or media enquiries.
  - Any policy with regard to closure of premises. Some organizations have a pre-printed notice which can be stuck in the window if an office or shop has to be closed. This informs the public why the premises have been closed and where the next nearest alternative can be found. It also has a secondary effect of reducing the number of adverse customer comments afterwards.
  - What to do if customers or members of the public are involved.
  - Any points regarding police enquiries, e.g. avoiding touching anywhere that the aggressor touched (so that forensic evidence such as fingerprints are not destroyed) or using the company or office address on witness statements (rather than an employee's home address); at a later date any statements may be read out and used in court (leaving staff fearful of some form of reprisal).
  - Informing any staff who were absent at the time of the incident. These people are easily overlooked and often only become aware of an incident through the media or when they return to work.
  - Any policy with regard to time off.
  - What help or support is available together with how this can be accessed.

- Where post-incident procedures require several actions involving a number of sources of information, it can be useful to bring them all together in an incident manual or file. Typically this would contain:
  - a checklist of actions required and points to be remembered
  - any documentation needed, e.g. incident report forms
  - a list of all important telephone numbers
  - any support materials, e.g. pre-printed notices for public information
  - a reminder to replenish any documents, notices or materials used
  - etc.
- Where the procedure concerns responding to burglary there are a few other important considerations. Usually the first indication that a burglary has taken place is either when the premises are opened at the start of the next working day by whoever arrives first, or by an alarm being triggered, or where obvious damage is noticed by someone and a key holder is called out (sometimes in the middle of the night). In particular the procedure should take into account:
  - the safety of any key holder who is called out (particularly during hours of darkness), e.g. recommending they do not attempt to enter any work premises until the police are present
  - taking care over opening work premises every morning (particularly in premises where there is a time-locked safe). There have been several incidents where assailants have been lying in wait for staff to arrive at work, as the following case study illustrates.

Case Study 7.2

As the manager of a small branch of a national building society, John made it a ritual to arrive at work early in order to open the office for the rest of the staff. On this particular day he arrived early as usual and entered by the front door. As he made his way towards his office he was distracted by a 'sticker' which presumably a child had stuck on the front of one of the counters. He stopped and tried to remove the sticker by scratching it with a key. However, while doing this he suddenly became aware of what looked like the top of a black hooded head at the other side of the counter. The sticker became irrelevant. John backed away and back out of the front door, his eyes glued on the counter in case the intruder decided to leap out.

John immediately notified the police, and stopped any other staff trying to get in. The whole incident became quite a spectacle. Armed police arrived and the building was surrounded. Finally when the police went in, the premises were empty but the back door was swinging wide open (with obvious marks on the frame where it had been forced open).

Although no one doubted that one or more intruders really had forced an entry into the branch, in the weeks that followed John found himself questioning whether he really did see anyone. Furthermore, if villains were there, why hadn't they jumped out and confronted him? However, John also recognized that if they had then the outcome could have been very different; for that he was thankful.

- One other important aspect of any procedure concerns 'designing in' measures for evaluating whether the procedure is:
  - practical and actually used
  - relevant
  - effective and useful for the individuals involved
  - cost effective for the organization

  As we will see later, evaluating the procedure through regular reviews is one way of ensuring this happens on a regular basis.

The case highlighted earlier also illustrates that in the aftermath of a serious incident there is generally a flurry of activity. As we saw in Chapter 6, the staff who were involved will still most likely be in shock and probably not thinking or acting normally. As a consequence it is very easy for them to overlook points of detail when trying to follow even the most simple procedure.

Ideally whoever coordinates what action is taken should be someone who was not themselves directly involved (as they are more likely to keep a level head). However, this may not be possible. In small offices or shops all of the staff may have been involved; similarly with staff on delivery duties, all of them may be victims. It is therefore important to provide some way of helping staff make sure that nothing is overlooked. Perhaps the simplest way of doing this is to provide a checklist which gives a complete list of all of the actions that need to be taken. Staff can then tick each item as soon as it has been carried out. An illustration is given in Fig. 7.1.

POST-INCIDENT CHECKLIST

Date of incident......................... Time............... Day of week............
Address where incident took place..
....
....

Action	Tick when completed
• First aid administered?	☐
• Medical assistance/ambulance called?	☐
• Support for anyone in distress arranged?	☐
• Police informed?	☐
• Head Office/Personnel/Security informed?	☐
• Partners/spouses/next of kin informed?	☐
• Premises closed?	☐
• Notice to public prominently displayed?	☐
• Damage repairs arranged?	☐
• Leaflets for victims distributed?	☐
• Assailant identification forms completed?	☐
• Incident report completed?	☐

Other notes ....
....
....

Figure 7.1   Illustration incident checklist

Although this may seem like an oversimplistic approach, it can be absolutely vital. What appears to be obvious when quietly reading a book bears no comparison with the mental processes of staff in the aftermath of a serious incident; a simple approach is essential.

Once formalized and agreed, the incident procedure will need to be communicated to staff. As with carrying out a survey of incidents, organizations which already have in place mechanisms for communicating with employees are at a real advantage. Finally, once the procedure is in place it will need regular rehearsal by the staff who need to use it and (as mentioned earlier in the point about evaluation) periodically reviewing. These will be the topics for the next two sections.

PROCEDURE REVIEWS

Reviews are an important way of evaluating the effectiveness of any procedure. However, practically everyone who has looked at this area agrees they are rarely carried out; even in the days after an incident few organizations review on a regular basis exactly what happened. Indeed, many victims report that once an incident has occurred, it is as if there is a conspiracy of silence surrounding the whole affair. No one wants to talk about what happened and what other, perhaps different, action should be taken next time.

If an organization wishes to establish whether a procedure has been effective then some form of review is essential. As mentioned earlier, this should seek to find out if the procedure was:

- Practical and actually used
- Relevant
- Effective and useful for the staff involved

Clearly this type of information can only be gathered after an incident has actually occurred. However, it must be made clear at the outset that the purpose of a procedure review is precisely that—

to review the effectiveness of the procedure. It is *not* a witch hunt. If, for any reason, individuals were unable to carry out the procedure there may be important reasons why not. If they fear castigation or disciplinary action then they may cover up or lie about how they actually behaved. This can suppress information which could be used to make the procedure more effective.

Equally it must be acknowledged that carrying out a review can bring back painful memories for those who were involved (particularly in organizations where personal support for employees is left to chance). Indeed, as an aside, this could be one of the reasons why post-incident reviews are comparatively rare. However, the fact that participating in a procedure review may be painful means that whoever carries out the review must do so sensitively. In fact it may be worth considering whether post-incident procedure reviews could become a part of more extensive de-briefing of staff after incidents. This type of de-briefing then serves two purposes. Firstly, it provides personal support for employees and, secondly, it provides information on the effectiveness of the procedure and at the same time actively demonstrates organizational concern. The precise format and structure of de-briefing will be discussed more fully later when we look specifically at follow-up and support.

Finally, in large organizations, any information gleaned from the procedure review element of de-briefing needs to be fed back to the central coordinator or coordinating group so that, where necessary, appropriate action can be taken. Although an obvious point, it is worth emphasizing that sometimes collecting information will lead to requests for further action. If no action follows then the review process will quickly fall into disrepute.

REGULAR PRACTICE

There is no point having a procedure if it is not well known by employees who may need to use it. Skills such as negative enquiry (for dealing with anger and abuse) can be acquired relatively quickly through a short training input, but are easily forgotten without regular practice. Similarly, what to do following a robbery or assault may be emphasized during induction training but without regular practice staff may find they have forgotten many of the details if an incident actually occurs. In a sense incident procedures are akin to learning first-aid; you are hopeful they are never needed, but thankful when they are.

In organizations the difficulty is judging how often is appropriate. On the one hand employees need to be conversant with how to respond, but at the same time there is no point in over-reacting so that they feel the procedure is being 'stuffed down their throats'. Equally, nationwide organizations may need to take account of geographical variations. Current trends in Britain suggest that procedures will be used much more often in London and the South East than elsewhere in the country. It follows, therefore, that employees who work in high-risk areas are likely to be using the procedure 'for real' on a more regular basis. Assuming that post-incident reviews are taking place, then to insist on regular practice as well could be perceived as overkill.

Nevertheless, this still leaves the problem of 'how often is appropriate?'. Having worked with organizations in finance, retail, delivery and social services, I would suggest a six month interval as an appropriate starting point. By this I mean either six months since the last practice (where no intervening incidents have taken place) or six months since the last incident took place (assuming post-incident reviews have taken place). The six month interval will then ensure that all staff receive regular updating and practice on what to do. Obviously in premises that are subject to incidents at more frequent intervals, staff will be using the procedure 'for real' even more often—in a few cases perhaps even as part of 'normal' working.

The detail of how regular practice can be carried out starts to overlap with preparation and training and will be discussed more fully later. In the meantime, it is probably more important to consider how to help staff cope while an incident is actually taking place.

HELPING STAFF DEVELOP PERSONAL COPING STRATEGIES

With aggressive or abusive incidents perhaps the best initial strategy is for staff to defuse the situation (as early as possible) using the skills outlined in Chapter 5. In most instances these will prove effective and the situation will not lead to open aggression or violence. However, in a minority of aggressive incidents and all criminal incidents (such as robbery and assault) some members of staff will inevitably become victims. Furthermore, when involved in an incident they commonly feel powerless and out of control. This is where personal coping strategies can be of enormous help. Staff who have developed coping strategies will generally have a much greater chance of being able to stay calm and in control of their own actions (despite the fact that they may have to comply with an assailant's demands). So what are personal coping strategies, how do they work and how can they be developed?

Personal coping strategies are simple personal messages or phrases which we learn to say to ourselves when under stress. Rather than allowing ourselves to be overwhelmed by feeling powerless it is possible to repeat to ourselves positive pre-prepared messages. They are a form of positive 'self-talk' or 'internal dialogue'. For example, during an incident it is possible for a victim to repeat silently personal messages or thoughts inside their head, e.g.:

- 'Stay calm.'
- 'Follow his instructions.'
- 'Don't panic.'
- 'This is not my fault.'
- 'Take note of his appearance.'

Although this strategy will not work in every case (sometimes the degree of trauma is simply too great), it will work in a large number of cases. Furthermore, it will help victims maintain some sense of control over their own actions and, at the same time, it will help reduce the psychological impact of an incident (and subsequently reducing the risk of PTSD developing).

However, before thinking about how personal coping strategies can be developed two further points need to be very heavily underlined:

1. They are *nothing* to do with 'having a go' or *in any way* encouraging victims to put themselves at risk. They involve private, silent thoughts—not physical action.
2. They involve personal phrases which individuals must develop for themselves. The phrases have to be in words that people create for themselves, i.e. words that feel comfortable.

Perhaps the easiest way for staff to develop a coping strategy is by taking part in an exercise where they are encouraged to think about (and list) the types of incidents that could occur in their workplace. Next, once the list is complete, taking one incident at a time, they use their imagination to visualize themselves being directly involved in such an incident. While doing this they should take note of what positive messages they would really like to be saying to themselves (or the assailant) at the time—no matter how strong or colourful. These are the coping phrases which will help in the event of an incident actually taking place. It follows, therefore, that they need to repeat their phrases over and over again so that they can be brought to mind automatically without even thinking.

Although this exercise might seem far-fetched and completely divorced from reality, it really does work. Staff who have thought about being involved in an incident and what they could say to themselves at the time tend to cope much better, and recover faster, than staff who have never thought about being involved in an incident (or, worse still, think it could never happen to them).

As we will see in Chapter 11, in one organization which uses this practice staff refer to their messages as their 'coping lines'. If it works, why discount it?

OTHER SELF-HELP TECHNIQUES

Using a personal coping strategy during an incident will help at the time the incident is taking place. Unfortunately, even though it will help to minimize the impact of an incident, victims may still experience disturbing post-incident effects. This is where a few other simple self-help skills can be of real value. However, before reading any further it may be worth trying out the following exercise.

Exercise 7.1
Think back to a period in your life when you felt under stress. With this in mind, make a list of all of the techniques and methods which helped you cope. When you have finished you might like to compare your ideas with those listed below.

Effective self-help techniques include all of the traditional stress management techniques listed below. As these have all been discussed at length by many other authors, this section will only point out how they can help with post-traumatic stress (for further information the reader should consult the texts suggested in Appendix 3, which gives a list of a few other useful publications).

Conscious relaxation

As we saw in Chapter 6, post-traumatic stress often results in a general increase in a victim's sense of anxiety. As a consequence, this usually leads to increased muscular tension. Conscious relaxation has the effect of counteracting tension by deliberate relaxation of muscle groups within the body. When practised regularly it will have the effect of gradually reducing anxiety, leaving victims (or anyone under stress) feeling more able to cope.

Physical exercise

People who exercise regularly generally feel more positive about life and, as a result, seem to be able to manage stress more easily.

Although simplistic, it is as if there is a link between physical fitness and mental resilience. This effect can be achieved with any form of exercise provided it raises heart rate and breathing for a sustained period, two or three times a week. (Note that anyone over the age of 40 should seek medical advice and/or a medical check-up before embarking on any exercise routine.)

Seeking Emotional Support

If a company has in place a support structure for victims as outlined in Chapter 8, then the emotional support component of stress management will be provided automatically. It is probably one of the most powerful stress management techniques. Furthermore, it is worth emphasizing again that most people can provide emotional support for victims provided they are prepared to listen to what a victim has to say without judging or criticizing them. This is the essence of emotional support; it does not require highly specialist skills (where needed Victim Support is available).

Diet

It has long been recognized that some foods act as stimulants (e.g. caffeine in coffee). It follows, therefore, that anyone who is suffering from anxiety should cut down or avoid food or drink which stimulates the system still further. In particular, victims suffering from post-traumatic stress should avoid excessive alcohol consumption (it is likely to make their condition worse rather than better).

Interests and hobbies

People who have no other interests or hobbies outside work often fare badly when their sense of security at work is undermined by involvement in a violent incident. By contrast, victims who have interests and concerns (which provide meaning to life) outside work can often find they provide a temporary haven while coming to terms with an incident at work. Involvement with an interest or hobby becomes in effect a sanctuary providing relief for a short period.

Note that it is important to emphasize that none of these techniques will provide a 'quick fix'. Unlike having a headache, where taking an aspirin or paracetamol will remove the pain quickly, post-traumatic stress is different. Nevertheless, when practised regularly, all of these techniques will help reduce anxiety, and in the longer term, help speed up recovery.

POST-INCIDENT PROCESSES

Finally, having looked at how staff can help themselves both during an incident and afterwards, it is important to be clear about the whole picture. Once an incident has taken place several different strands of activity are set in motion and these have important implications for both the design of training and the structure of follow-up and support.

Following an incident (and in particular with serious incidents) up to four different processes may take place concurrently. Firstly, the staff who were directly involved will be going through their own individual recovery process (as described in Chapter 6); secondly, there may be some form of audit and/or security procedure which is set in motion; thirdly, there may be police investigatory procedures and, subsequently, judicial processes which have to take place; fourthly, insurance and/or compensation inquiries may be set in motion. A schematic diagram illustrating all of these is given in Fig. 7.2.

Although all of these strands of activity are quite separate from one another, they do affect each other. For example, as was mentioned in Chapter 6, some aspects of assisting with police investigations and being summoned to give evidence in court can cause a relapse in an individual's recovery. Similarly, audit and security inquiries can cause equally significant setbacks. As we turn our attention towards follow-up, support and training, it is

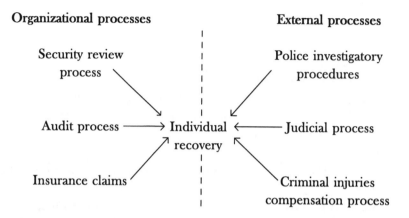

Figure 7.2   Processes that can affect an individual's recovery

important to be aware of these processes and their potential impact on the people involved. In turn this will affect both when and where and how follow-up and support is provided and the content of any training.

SUMMARY

- Responding effectively can involve:
  - designing and implementing appropriate organizational procedures
  - training and re-training of staff at regular intervals
  - implementing post-incident procedure reviews
  - providing follow-up and support for staff who may have been involved
- Procedure should seek to:
  - minimize the degree of risk for individuals
  - provide some measure of psychological security
  - minimize any goods or money stolen
- Post-incident procedures must be kept as simple as possible.
- Post-incident reviews are an important way of evaluating the

effectiveness of any procedure. They should seek to establish whether the procedure was:
- practical and actually used
- relevant
- effective and useful for the staff involved
- Because of the difficulties involved, it may be worth considering whether post-incident procedure reviews could become part of a more extensive de-briefing of staff after incidents.
- Procedures need to be practised regularly, e.g. every six months.
- Staff who have developed a personal coping strategy will generally have a much greater chance of staying calm and in control when an incident takes place.
- Developing a personal coping strategy requires staff to imagine what positive messages they would like to say to themselves when confronted by an assailant. Once committed to memory these phrases become a powerful way of minimizing the psychological impact of an incident.
- Other self-help techniques include relaxation, regular physical exercise, emotional support, having external interests/hobbies and attention to diet.
- In order to provide appropriate training and/or follow-up and support it is important to take account of all of the processes that could affect victims.

8

Follow-up and support

INTRODUCTION

Following involvement in an incident staff will often need additional follow-up and support beyond implementation of an immediate response procedure. Although some people do seem to be very resilient and appear largely unaffected (even by very traumatic incidents), they are the exception. Indeed, one could argue that the success of organizations like Victim Support is testimony to the fact that victims of crime need help. Regardless of whether incidents take place at home, at work or elsewhere, victims (and sometimes witnesses) may need additional help. Furthermore, with incidents at work, it is important for staff to see their employer taking such incidents seriously. I believe it is vital that initial sources of help are rooted in the workplace; other external help should be seen to be complementary. However, having said this it is important to ask, 'What kind of help is effective?'

Yet again the answer is not simple. It will depend on the type of incident, the organizational resources available, the individual involved and the impact of any subsequent inquiries. Following from this, it would appear that (where possible) a flexible approach is needed. Ideally this will be geared to the needs of the individual (and, as pointed out earlier, the degree of variation in individual reactions can be enormous). Nevertheless, despite this I would like to suggest that follow-up and support can be broken into three main stages:

- Immediate post-incident emergency support

- Individual follow-up and/or group de-briefing
- Longer term individual support (where needed)

The rest of this chapter will examine each of these stages in detail.

POST-INCIDENT EMERGENCY SUPPORT

Post-incident emergency support is about what happens in the first few hours after an incident has taken place. Clearly the detail of how this support is provided will vary from one setting to another. For example, with aggression and verbal abuse it may be adequate for other staff (or a manager) to step in and provide any help that is needed. However, with more serious incidents it may be necessary to close the business for a few hours and call in relief staff. Nevertheless, the main objectives at this stage are to:

- Provide immediate help and support for any staff who are affected by the incident and
- Ensure the organization gets back into normal operation as soon as practicable

Generally, achieving these objectives does not require specialists to be involved. After training any of the following groups should be able to provide appropriate help:

- Other colleagues who were at the scene of the incident but were not themselves directly affected
- Other staff (e.g. security, personnel or more senior managers) who are called in as part of the post-incident procedure
- A 'standby team' of staff from other locations who are called in to take over the running of the operation

The crucial point to bear in mind is that staff are affected by incidents both personally and in terms of carrying out their work. Having an effective emergency response makes sense on commercial grounds alone.

With respect to providing personal support, anyone who is

involved with the emergency response will need to be well versed in helping people in shock. Indeed, with very serious incidents staff may be severely traumatized. In such circumstances a response which simply concentrates on getting the business up and running again may be seen as callous and inhuman. Staff needs must be addressed as well.

However, before discussing these in detail, try to complete the following exercise to check out your own level of knowledge concerning helping people who are in shock:

Exercise 8.1
Imagine one of your colleagues at work has just been subjected to serious verbal abuse by an angry customer. The customer has now left the premises and your colleague has fled to a back office clearly very distressed. On a separate sheet of paper make a list of what actions you would take to provide personal support.

When you have finished carry on by tackling the following:

Now imagine the same or a similar incident once again, but this time imagine it involved either violent or armed assault. Although your colleague was not physically injured he or she was extremely distressed as a result. What additional action would you take under these circumstances? Add them to your list.

When you have finished, compare your ideas with those discussed below.

Chapter 6 pointed out that shock affects different people in different ways. Nevertheless, there are a few general guidelines for providing help. These are listed in the following checklist for providing immediate post-incident support:

- Encourage the individual(s) to talk about what happened and how they felt.
- Acknowledge and affirm that what they are experiencing is normal.
- Use listening skills to help them talk.
- Do not get caught up in apportioning blame.
- Guard against using any casual or throwaway remark that could be perceived as hurtful.

- Ensure that victims (or witnesses) who are affected are accompanied for as long as needed—even if they are taken away from the workplace (e.g. taken to a police station).
- Encourage early contact with anyone else who was involved in the incident.
- As soon as appropriate, encourage victims to return to the scene of the incident (though obviously do *not* apply any unnecessary pressure).
- As soon as appropriate, provide relevant information on what will happen next and how the victim may be involved, e.g. police, internal security or managerial interviews, etc. Providing this type of practical support can be just as important as emotional support.

Additionally, with more serious incidents:

- Keep next of kin and/or relatives informed about what is happening and where the person is located (e.g. at work, police station, hospital, etc.). However, do check out with the victim who they wish to be informed and when. Even though the company may have a list of 'next of kin', this might not be up to date, or indeed, reflect what a victim would want. For example, a young adult may have nominated a parent as their next of kin, but they may well wish to retain control over how and when the parent is told (or there may be other people in their lives who they would wish to be informed first). Finally, do bear in mind that relatives are likely to become anxious or upset as well and may themselves require support.
- Ensure that lifts and transport are arranged for victims and/or witnesses and their relatives. In particular, *do not* allow them to drive home while in a state of shock.
- Ensure that victims do not go home to an empty house. If necessary stay with them until a relative arrives.
- If those affected are likely to need any time off, then affirm that this will be acceptable, but do not encourage long spells of absence.
- Advise against taking any unprescribed sleeping pills or other medication.

- If necessary (and in particular with people who may be adversely affected by shock) encourage them to visit their GP.
- Inform both the person and any close relatives what other help is available and how it can be accessed. Some organizations have produced a brief leaflet to be given to victims following an incident. Typically these highlight what kind of reactions to expect, what to do (and not do), together with where to go for further help. This can be excellent back-up material for post-incident support. (Note that even if a company has its own internal support system it could be worth including in any literature a section on, 'how to contact external sources of help' (including Victim Support). Some staff victims may prefer to approach an external body themselves so that their referral and request for help is not known by anyone in the company.)
- Above all, encourage anyone who is affected to talk about their experience and how they feel. As a general rule, suggesting that victims should bottle-up their feelings is not helpful. Very often this belief is based on the following myth.

'People should not be asked or reminded about an incident if it upsets them.'

It is not unusual for both victims and witnesses to become upset when recounting abusive or aggressive incidents. Furthermore, I would wager that anyone who has experienced a potentially violent or life-threatening situation is likely to be disturbed when talking about it (particularly during the first few hours after the incident has taken place). However, this does not mean avoiding discussing the subject. Quite the contrary, not allowing victims to talk through their experience can be positively harmful. It will generally leave them feeling isolated and, in some cases, believing they failed in some way, despite being involved in an event that was largely out of their control. If this continues it can lead to serious complications later.

Encouraging victims to talk about their experience may well mean they become anxious and/or upset. As a consequence this means that support staff who are involved in the immediate aftermath of an incident should expect the people who are involved to be distressed. This is usually the norm rather than the exception. Acknowledging and accepting their distress is far more helpful than suggesting they should 'pull themselves together'. Victims come to terms with their experience by facing and accepting what happened (painful though it is), and realizing their reaction is perfectly normal. However, having stated this, it is also important to emphasize that victims must be allowed to come to terms with their experience in their own time. They cannot and should not be rushed. Sometimes the full impact of an incident may not be experienced until several hours later, perhaps when they are at home. It follows therefore that another important aspect of providing support involves forewarning relatives that this sometimes happens.

Before leaving this section perhaps it would be wise to add a note of caution with respect to using a 'standby team' to ensure that a business gets back into operation quickly. While commercially this option may appear attractive (particularly in large organizations where other staff can be drawn in quickly), it can present an additional difficulty. For victims, a relief team can exacerbate their sense of feeling powerless and out of control. Furthermore, where premises have been closed and are reopened very quickly, it can be perceived by permanent staff as an insult to their experience. Although perhaps difficult to understand, it is as if stopping operations for a while is perceived as a mark of respect to the victims who have been abused.

Obviously companies want to minimize any operational losses as a result of incidents, but this does need to be balanced against any effects on members of staff. Where it is company policy to resume operations as quickly as possible it would be wise to ensure that staff are informed this will happen during initial training. Then at least when the policy is put into effect it will not come as a surprise.

As an aside, it is important to stress that workplace support should be seen to be automatic and simply an expression of organizational concern, rather than a 'knee-jerk' response to a 'problem'. 'Good practice' must include staff support as a part of normal organizational life.

Finally, it is worth noting that in many cases (particularly those which involve abuse and aggression rather than serious trauma) the immediate post-incident support may be all the help that victims need. Giving them the opportunity to talk through their experience may be quite enough. Where this seems to be the case it is probably sensible to go along with the victim's wishes. However, it would also be sensible to make sure they receive an informal telephone call or conversation a few days later to check whether they really are feeling fine and not attempting to suppress more deeply felt distress.

By contrast, with more serious incidents follow-up and support is, in my view, essential.

APPROACHES TO FOLLOW-UP AND SUPPORT

Many organizations have arrangements in place for emergency support following incidents at work (particularly more serious, traumatic incidents). After all there are often obvious commercial interests at stake when business is disrupted and/or premises closed. However, once the business is up and running again the commercial impact of the longer term suffering of staff is less obvious. Yet despite this, a number of larger organizations are now beginning to provide follow-up, de-briefing and longer term support for staff. They recognize that incidents at work affect both the morale and performance of staff (as well as pushing up sickness absence figures). As a result, several different approaches have been adopted, these include:

- Using 'in-house' full-time professional counsellors to deal with all cases
- Using one or two full-time professional counsellors primarily

as coordinators (and to deal with more serious cases), with the bulk of support being carried out by a network of trained peer supporters/counsellors (i.e. ordinary members of staff—usually volunteers who have received special training)
- Extending the role of other specialist staff and providing them with appropriate additional training (e.g. welfare officers, occupational health nurses/advisers, etc.)
- Using line managers, personnel or security staff
- Using an external consultant counsellor or counselling agency (e.g. organizations offering an Employee Assistance Programme).

Given this range of approaches it may be useful to spend a few minutes thinking about the relative advantages, disadvantages and difficulties of each.

Exercise 8.2
Glance back at the list of approaches to helping staff and select one which you feel would be appropriate for your organization. If your organization already uses one particular approach then use that one for the purpose of this exercise.

Once you have an approach clearly in mind, then on a separate sheet of paper make a list of the relative advantages, disadvantages and any other points worth noting (both for victims and for the company). When you have finished, compare your ideas with the discussion that follows.

Using 'in-house' full-time professional counsellors for all cases

Advantages
- Offers an 'in-house' professional service for all staff (and their families?) who are involved in an incident.
- Other than where physical injuries are sustained, outside referrals will be rare.
- The counselling service can also be opened up to offer more general workplace counselling.
- Expertise can be used in other directions, e.g. in training, as a

source of help with other organizational issues such as introducing major change.
- Able to offer feedback/advice to senior management on staff concerns (however, care will be needed to avoid breaching individual confidentiality).

Disadvantages
- Expensive. Costs will include direct wages and overheads, confidential administrative back-up, professional supervision (which is usually external), ongoing personal training and development for counsellors.
- Unless strict boundaries are agreed on either the type of cases dealt with or the number of interviews normally offered, then the demand for the service is likely to grow like 'Topsy' (particularly where more general workplace counselling is offered).
- The service may be used as an excuse by managers and staff for not becoming involved with victims (or other employees who need counselling) on a day-to-day basis, i.e. they may perceive it as 'not my job'.
- In some cases the counselling service may become a 'political' tool when major change is being imposed.

Points worth noting
- Where counselling is located within an organizational framework will have implications for how the service is perceived by staff. The usual locations are either attached to personnel, occupational health or welfare. However, each sends out different messages depending on the 'track record' of that particular department.
- Even in organizations where no formal support for victims is offered, introducing a counselling service needs to be carried out sensitively. Almost inevitably some staff (e.g. individual personnel officers or welfare officers) will have tried to offer help on an informal basis and, with the introduction of a formal service, may feel 'pushed out'. It is far better to find out

beforehand who these people are and to harness their support.

- Professional counsellors within an organization tend to be few in number. Usually there is no way of providing an internal career structure for them.

Using one or two full-time professional counsellors as coordinators of volunteer peer/staff supporters

Advantages

- Assuming volunteers have been appropriately selected and trained, this approach offers an effective service together with 'in-house' professional expertise when needed.
- External referrals will be more common than where professional counsellors deal with all cases, but they will still be comparatively rare.
- Expertise may be used in other ways, though the time available for this could quickly become limited.
- Assuming there is good communication with volunteer supporters, the coordinator should be able to offer feedback to senior management on general staff concerns.

Disadvantages

- Again, this can be used by managers and staff as an excuse for refusing to become involved with victims on a day-to-day basis.
- This is an extremely demanding role for the coordinator. It requires a very wide range of skills, e.g. professional counselling for severe cases, casework supervisor for peer counsellors, trainer for ensuring peer counsellors are adequately trained, advocate/negotiator on behalf of peer counsellors, skills required for any other duties, etc.
- The need to offer a completely confidential service can lead to organizational isolation and lack of support. This will also be exacerbated in aggressively competitive organizations where all departments regularly have to 'prove their worth'.
- In very large organizations that have outlets or offices across a

wide geographical area it can be very difficult for the coordinator to prevent regional variations in how the service is delivered.

Points worth noting
- The network of peer counsellors will need to match the geographic spread of the organization. However, the concentration of incidents in particular areas will often mean that counsellors in other areas are likely to be less frequently used. As a consequence particular efforts will have to be made to ensure they maintain their skills.
- In order that peer counsellors do not feel 'used' the organization will need to consider and reach an agreement on a whole range of administrative details, e.g. remuneration/reward for work carried out, where and when counselling takes place, (i.e. in office hours or after hours, on work premises or at a victim's home?), transport arrangements and expenses for counsellors, etc.

Expanding the role of existing specialist staff
Advantages
- Requires no new appointment of staff.
- Will often be seen by existing staff as a natural expansion of the work that specialists carry out. Indeed, in large organizations where such specialists are employed, no doubt they will have already been trying to offer help to victims anyway.
- This approach harnesses, uses and extends the existing credibility and contacts of specialist staff without introducing any dramatic new arrangements.

Disadvantages
- Will require external specialist help for ongoing back-up and support with more serious cases and is likely to lead to more external referrals for help.
- In order to exist today most organizations have become 'lean

and hungry'. Where specialist services still exist they are generally stretched to the limit. As a consequence, taking on this type of role expansion may be too much. Specialists may feel it is important to offer a victim support service but find, in practice, it is not possible. The demand for their services from other quarters may be simply too great.

- Unless someone takes a central coordination role, feedback to senior management will be difficult to organize.

Points worth noting

- Specialist staff (particularly occupational health and welfare officers) often become involved with victims during the course of their normal work. Given appropriate training and external specialist support, formally extending their role to include follow-up and support of victims is generally welcomed.

Using line managers, personnel or security staff

Advantages

- Requires no new appointments of staff.
- Most managers, personnel and security staff are intensely concerned when colleagues become victims of violent crime at work. Encouraging them to become more directly involved in offering support to victims often permits them to demonstrate their concern more directly.
- Managers who have undergone training for supporting victims report that the skills needed also have widespread application in day-to-day management.
- In instances where managers have provided support for staff it often consolidates and further develops the relationship between them.

Disadvantages

- Will require external specialist help for ongoing back-up and support with more serious cases and is likely to lead to considerably more external referrals for help.

- As with expanding the role of other specialists, managers, personnel and security staff might also find that because of other pressures, in practice they have little time to devote to victims.
- Follow-up and support of victims necessarily involves offering a completely confidential service. Victims may experience very real difficulty in trusting managers or personnel officers to this degree because of their primary role within the company. As a consequence victims may be fearful of disclosing anything that could be perceived as weakness and self-censor what they say or, alternatively, refuse to accept help altogether (even though it may be desperately needed).
- Managers, personnel officers or security staff might not want to take on this kind of responsibility simply because of their role in the company. Despite any training offered they may feel ill equipped and 'out of their depth' when dealing with colleagues who may become distressed.

Points worth noting
- Even where an organization opts to use a different approach, support and day-to-day concern from personnel, security staff and especially line managers is invaluable. Over and above support and concern from staff who are employed to look after victims, line managers are in a position to demonstrate that organizational concern means far more than simply words written in a procedure. They can show that it also extends into everyday behaviour.

Using an external counsellor or counselling agency
Advantages
- Requires no new appointments of internal staff.
- An effective external counsellor or agency can offer a professional and highly confidential follow-up and support service for all staff.
- Generally contractual arrangements on how the service will

operate can be agreed to suit both the organization and individual victims.

- If required, and assuming contractual arrangements are agreed, the service could be broadened into more general workplace counselling.

Disadvantages
- Offers no opportunity for development of internal staff. Indeed, the imposition of an external agency may act as a deterrent to staff who wish to offer support.
- Feedback to senior management is often possible but it will not have the same degree of organizational awareness as that which can be provided by an internal system.
- Places overall control for how victims are helped outside the organization.

Points to note
- Remuneration of external agencies will inevitably highlight the costs of longer term support. This can be a mixed blessing. On the one hand it can confront an organization with part of the cost of violence, yet on the other hand it can also accelerate demands for a line to be drawn. For victims this could mean ill-health/medical retirement.

Before closing this section it is worth pointing out that all of the approaches to follow-up and support that have been discussed so far are mainly relevant to large (or very large) organizations. Yet small companies are just as prone to violence and crime as any other (perhaps even more so, as in smaller companies there are often few other staff around when an incident takes place). The following section will therefore address the particular needs of victims in small organizational settings.

SUPPORT FOR SMALL ORGANIZATIONS

Violence and crime against small businesses is of particular concern. A study of small retail shops by Hibbard and Shapland[15] in London and the West Midlands found that in London a quarter of the sample had experienced robbery (or attempted robbery) within the last twelve months, and one in six in the Midlands. Additionally, more than a third in the Midlands and just over a quarter in London reported experiencing general violence and argumentativeness. Of those in the sample who were Asian over 30 per cent in both locations reported racial abuse; furthermore, this was perceived as a regular occurrence rather than isolated incidents.

There are several reasons why small businesses are a special case. Firstly, these types of businesses are often family run, hence being a victim of violence and crime immediately becomes a family issue. Any losses sustained will be personal loss rather than an employer's loss. Often the people involved are unable to take any sick leave even though it may be badly needed; if they did the business simply could not function. By definition, small businesses do not have extensive managerial structures or specialists on hand who may be able to provide post-incident support. Furthermore, many do not have the resources to install expensive security equipment which could help deter future incidents. Hence, support for small businesses is a very real concern.

Anne Viney of Victim Support highlights a number of self-help strategies[16] which may be useful for a small business owner if a member of his or her family (or an employee) becomes a victim of violence and crime. They include:

- Showing concern about the impact of the incident on both the victim and the family.
- Asking how they felt and encouraging them to talk about their current feelings.
- Making time to talk, either face-to-face or by telephone.
- Encouraging peer support within business groups or through trade/professional associations.
- Making sure people have time to talk to one another—and above all listening.

- Avoiding blaming. Victims often blame themselves, but this does not need compounding by blame from others. Victims need to be reassured that they did the best they could under the circumstances.

Where additional help is needed then clearly it must be sought from external sources within the wider community, e.g.:

- Approaching a local branch of Victim Support. Their telephone number can be found in the telephone directory or from directory enquiries or from the police. A branch of Victim Support is available in most areas and their volunteers are specifically trained in helping victims of violence. Furthermore, they now operate a widespread witness support service for people who are required to give evidence in court.
- Seeking help through the victim's own GP. The GP is the primary source of care in the community. Nowadays many are starting to retain or establish contact with one or more local counsellors who may be able to help. Although such counsellors might not be specifically trained in working with victims of crime, they will certainly be able to offer a professional counselling service.
- Buying in the services of a local counsellor or counselling agency on a 'one-off' basis. Counselling services are occasionally advertised in the local press; alternatively the British Association for Counselling may be able to help (their address is given in Appendix 1 along with other useful addresses).
- Approaching the Samaritans. Although the Samaritans themselves do not offer specific help for victims of violence and crime, they will be prepared to offer support, and, if required, long term support, to anyone who is in need. They are a national organization and have branches in most major cities and towns. The telephone number of a local branch can be found from the telephone directory or directory enquiries.
- The Council for Voluntary Services (CVS). The CVS will not be able to offer any direct help themselves; however, they do

keep a register of voluntary organizations within their particular locality. Hence they may be able to provide a bridge to other local organizations that may be able to provide some form of help/support. Again, the telephone number of any local CVS will be found in the telephone directory or through directory enquiries.

In general it is fair to say that the needs of victims of crime are becoming more widely recognized within the general community. However, other than organizations like Victim Support and a few others in the voluntary sector, together with some healthcare professionals, little else is available for smaller companies. Perhaps this is therefore an appropriate forum to suggest that some initiative from bodies such as Chambers of Commerce or Trade Associations would be a welcome addition for providing further support to the small business community. This could take the form of awareness raising activities, training or more direct help with victims of crime in the small company. Either way, given the incidence of crime today, there is a very real need for some group or organization to lead the way.

WHAT DOES FOLLOW-UP AND SUPPORT INVOLVE?

Practitioners who regularly work with victims are unanimous in pointing out that victims need to be offered follow-up, support and an opportunity to verbalize how they feel. The absence of this type of help can sometimes lead to more serious problems later. This leads to an important question, 'Should help be offered in a proactive manner or simply be available if victims care to ask?' Personally I favour the former. In my view support should be offered proactively as a matter of course. If an organization waits for victims to ask for help then very few are likely to put themselves forward. Regardless of what is said to the contrary, victims will most likely perceive asking for help as a sign of weakness which could have a detrimental effect on their career or employment. From an organizational point of view, waiting for victims to ask for help simply does not work.

As mentioned earlier, I believe that offering help needs to become a normal everyday organizational action after an incident has taken place. The more an organization can project a message that staff may (or may not) be affected by violent incidents and that their reactions are normal (rather than any personal weakness), the easier it will be for them to recover from the experience. Within the organization, offering help should become simply one expression of 'the way we do things here'.

However, at the other extreme, victims should not be pressurized into accepting help. Support needs to be offered in such a way that victims are free to accept or decline without fear of any stigma being attached either way. Following a model developed by Victim Support, the main purpose of this type of service is to offer:

- Confidential emotional support
- Practical help
- Appropriate/relevant information

In practice this can mean:

- Offering victims an opportunity to talk in confidence about what happened and how they felt
- Being prepared to listen actively to help victims talk about their experience without criticizing or judging them
- Sometimes outlining the range of reactions that people normally experience after a traumatic incident
- If necessary providing information or practical help on completing any forms or documents
- Helping victims help themselves to come to terms with their experience
- Providing information and help with any points that victims may have overlooked or not thought about
- Offering further follow-up if needed

This model of helping individual victims can be transferred directly into most organizational settings. Given appropriate training (which will be discussed in Chapter 9) and supervision, it can be delivered by colleagues, supervisors, managers or specialist staff. Not only will it prove effective in helping victims come to terms with their experience but it will also help to minimize some of the organizational costs highlighted in Chapter 3. Furthermore, it is a style of helping that can be carried out either at work (in a private office) or in the victim's own home.

It is important to make sure that help is offered to everyone who was involved in an incident, i.e.:

- Victims themselves.
- Any witnesses who may be affected.
- In particular it is important not to overlook any part-time staff or staff who may have been on loan from another office.

There is no doubt that helping victims in this way is highly effective. However, in some settings it may be more appropriate to organize group de-briefing (particularly in instances where an incident affected a group of staff who work together). To be effective group de-briefing needs to be carried out within two or three days of an incident taking place. Typically the entire group who were involved (including witnesses) are brought together in a private room with a de-briefing leader who is trained to facilitate this type of meeting. Typically the de-briefing process follows a number of sequential stages.

Introduction

At the start of the de-briefing the leader outlines the purpose of the meeting, why it is taking place and what it seeks to achieve. Next he or she lays down a number of important basic ground rules, e.g.

- That the meeting must be entirely confidential. No matter what is said, any disclosures made during the de-briefing will not be reported or discussed elsewhere.

- Similarly, taking notes or using any other form of recording is not allowed.

Finally, the leader also affirms that everyone present was involved in the incident in one capacity or another.

Establishing the facts

Following the introduction, it is important next to establish exactly what happened and what everyone was doing when the incident took place. This means inviting everyone at the de-briefing to share their perception of the experience and (as far as possible) try to reach some agreement over what actually happened. The intention at this stage is primarily to help clarify everyone's role as the incident took place.

Establishing what everyone was thinking and sensing

The next stage involves a discussion of the thoughts and sensory impressions of all those who were involved. In particular, it is important to bring to light (and if necessary challenge) any intrusive thoughts that staff may be experiencing. For example, it is not unusual for staff who witnessed an incident to feel unnecessarily guilty or start to believe they should have done more to help colleagues who were directly involved. When such thoughts become distortions of what actually happened they need to be challenged. It is very important not to allow distortions of reality to take hold in someone's mind; they can be detrimental and lead to a negative spiral.

Similarly, sensory impressions can be equally intrusive. They can take many forms:

- Where victims have been touched or manhandled by an assailant, they may feel an overwhelming sense of revulsion, as if they were contaminated in some way.
- Sometimes visual impressions persist, e.g. the flash of a blade or the black hole of a gun barrel.

- Where firearms have been discharged, the intrusive memory may be auditory. Even trained police officers are sometimes taken by surprise by the level of noise made by a gun being fired in a confined space. Similarly, anyone who has witnessed a weapon being tested will probably remember (above all else) the sound of the explosion as it was fired.
- Occasionally the memory may concern smell—perhaps after-shave or body odour where a victim (or witness) came into close proximity with an assailant. Equally, sometimes smells may concern everyday odours that just happened to coincide with the time when the incident took place.

All of these sensory impressions can lead to debilitating intrusive memories which, if not discussed, can become distorted and out of control in the victim's mind.

Establishing emotional reactions

Discussing emotional reactions is personally the most demanding phase for any facilitator/de-briefing leader. He or she must observe staff reactions very carefully and be prepared to follow up after the meeting with any member of the group who seemed unusually quiet or appeared to be experiencing a particularly severe reaction. Similarly group de-briefing will need careful handling where there is disagreement about the incident or the way it was handled. In such cases staff may not share the same reactions.

However, while having added these words of caution, it is also important to point out that during the discussion of emotional reactions, people generally discover that their reactions are similar to those of others who were involved. This is one of the great benefits of group de-briefing. Victims and/or witnesses can begin to realize that their own private, personal experience is not exceptional; it is also shared (in part) by others who were involved. Although this realization does not take away any of the pain of the experience, in a strange way it does become easier. Emotional reactions and mental pain do ease when shared with others who went through the same experience.

Normalizing the experience and providing anticipatory guidance and advice

In practical terms normalizing an experience is where the de-briefing leader summarizes all the thoughts, impressions and emotional reactions of everyone who was involved. In particular he or she emphasizes where reactions were shared and highlights the normality of their experience.

This is a crucial stage in the whole de-briefing process. It is essential that everyone who was involved has a chance to express how they feel and (if necessary) receive help in recognizing that their reaction is perfectly normal. In cases where this does not take place, victims will feel isolated and cut off from everyone else; in extreme cases, they may even become fearful that they are having a breakdown.

However, once the experience has been normalized, the group leader can move on to providing anticipatory guidance and advice. Effectively this aims to prepare people who are affected for what happens in the future. It could include:

- Providing basic information and advice on any further possible reactions as time passes—at the same time emphasizing that this is normal.
- Where cases may end up in court, pointing out what effects to expect as a result of police investigations and judicial processes.
- Where appropriate, providing relevant information concerning what to do to pursue claims for compensation.
- Giving guidance on self-help techniques such as stress management.
- Providing information about external sources of help.

It is also worth remembering that guidance, advice and information may have to be given in small chunks. Even though everyone will have had a chance to discuss their experience, they still might not be in the right frame of mind to take in all the information at once. Indeed, it could be worth summarizing any advice in a written checklist which can be given out at the end of the de-briefing.

Planning for the future

Planning for the future is about helping people think through how they can turn anticipatory advice into a plan of action. Yet again this stage is important; when carried out properly action planning starts to empower those who were involved in the incident to help themselves. Often this is in sharp contrast to the sense of powerlessness they may have experienced during the incident. However, empowerment can only happen in an environment that is sensitive to the impact of violence and crime on people. Where this is not evident, in my view it begs important questions for the culture of the organization and the role of training.

Disengagement

Disengagement marks the end of group de-briefing. For many it will be all that is needed; however, sometimes a minority of people will need further help. It therefore follows that during de-briefing it is important finally to point out what additional sources of longer term support are available. This will be the topic for the next major section.

Finally, before leaving support and de-briefing, it is important to mention that this description of the de-briefing process is based on work carried out by Dyregrov with helpers in disaster situations.[17] Although at first sight a disaster may appear to have little in common with violence and crime at work, the common feature is exposure to a traumatic event. As a consequence, at a general level, the symptoms and reactions which those involved experience are remarkably similar. Indeed, it is worth emphasizing that the types of support described here can be equally useful for providing general help to victims and witnesses in other types of traumatic situations. Furthermore, although relatively infrequent by comparison with violence and crime at work, a surprising variety of traumatic incidents do affect employees from time to time (some organizations and groups more than others), e.g.:

- Train drivers who are in charge of a train when it collides with someone who commits suicide by standing or jumping on to the track. Since the advent of North Sea Gas (which is not actually poisonous), jumping in front of a train has become a more common means of committing suicide. As a result many drivers have been badly affected.
- Serious/horrific road traffic accidents can be very disturbing for any driver or onlooker who just happens to be present when the accident takes place.
- Although rarely part of the headlines, large-scale disasters also have organizational consequences: e.g. the Piper Alpha disaster involved a number of Gardner Merchant staff who were working offshore at the time; the fire and police services were obviously involved with both the Kings Cross and Bradford Football Club fires—in both instances some officers were very seriously affected; flight officers and cabin staff could not avoid involvement in the Kegworth and Manchester air disasters; many of the victims and bystanders at Hillsborough, although spectators at a football match, were also employees of a whole range of different organizations (not to mention officers of the South Yorkshire Police who cleared up the carnage and carried the corpses of those who did not survive to a temporary mortuary).

Clearly, because of the relative infrequency of large-scale disasters, it is generally not worth an organization setting up a support structure specifically to help in such cases. However, although this is a specialist area and requires specialist skills, a support structure for helping victims of violence and crime can prove equally useful in providing general support for employees who have been affected by other forms of trauma.

LONGER TERM SUPPORT

An effective emergency response followed by either individual support or group de-briefing coupled with a sensitive organizational culture will generally satisfy most victims' needs. However, sadly there will inevitably be a few people who will need longer term help. Indeed, a few of these may find they are unable to return to work at all.

People who fall into either of these categories will usually be very seriously affected and probably suffering from severe post-traumatic stress disorder. Typically they will need specialist help and will probably be absent from work for some time (perhaps even several months). Here there may be a need for some form of assessment—usually medical and/or psychological assessment—to advise on the longer term prognosis. Yet even where this is the case it is important for colleagues and other staff from work to maintain contact. In this respect the following myth is very relevant.

'When people are absent from work following an incident, it is better to leave them alone to come to terms with their experience—outside interference can make their suffering worse.'

Not maintaining contact with victims who are absent from work for an extended period following an incident is like a form of organizational solitary confinement. Regardless of whatever action is taken during the first few days, ongoing contact *must* be maintained. Even when victims are suffering from severe post-traumatic stress disorder contact with workmates, colleagues, supervisors and/or managers can be helpful.

The only way anyone from a victim's workplace can exacerbate their condition is by trivializing or discounting their experience. In my experience, colleagues, friends and managers rarely, if ever, act in this way.

By way of straight advice, I would recommend that anyone who knows a colleague who has been involved in a traumatic incident and is absent from work, should make contact now. Simply remember a few simple guidelines:

- Allow them to talk.
- Listen without judging or criticizing.
- Never trivialize, minimize or discount their experience.
- Never offer advice about what they should do next.

and

- Above all, listen (and show that you are listening).

Even in instances where a member of staff never returns to work (and may be retired on ill-health grounds), ongoing contact with colleagues is important. It will invariably help ease their exit from the organization. Although this is a very sensitive area, sometimes it is the most appropriate way of helping victims who have been very seriously affected by an incident and, as a result, cannot return to their particular occupation. They should be offered an honourable and dignified way of leaving the company. This should acknowledge what they have experienced rather than covertly forcing them to resign.

A second group of staff who may need longer term support are those who become involved with police and judicial procedures. Typically this means taking part in an identity parade and/or appearance in court. As we have seen earlier, both of these procedures can prove to be harrowing experiences for even the most stalwart victim. However, being accompanied by a colleague (or friend) who is prepared to listen and be with the victim both before and after either experience can make all the difference. Although a colleague cannot take away the anxiety which the victim will feel during the experience, they can help them put it in perspective afterwards. Once again, it is worth mentioning that where this kind of support cannot be arranged internally within a company it may be worth seeking the help of the Victim Support Witness Service.

WHEN TO SEEK PROFESSIONAL HELP

Chapter 6 highlighted the fact that the vast majority of victims do not need professional help. Indeed, most of the approaches to providing support discussed earlier in this chapter rely on colleagues, supervisors, managers or other specialists (such as personnel, occupational health or security). In fact only the larger organizations can even contemplate employing a professional counsellor (and even then he or she will probably provide professional supervision and act as back-up to a network of peer counsellors).

Nevertheless, it is a fact that sometimes victims will need to be referred for professional help. It follows, therefore, that any non-professionals who are involved with helping victims will need to have a clear understanding of when and where to seek further help. Before discussing this in any detail, try to complete the following exercise to help you clarify your own thinking on this matter.

Exercise 8.3
Assuming you are not a trained counsellor, imagine that part of your role at work involves providing support for victims of violence and crime. Think for a moment about the more serious cases you might encounter, then on a separate sheet of paper write down as many instances as you can think of where you would seek more professional help. When you have finished you might like to compare your response with the discussion that follows.

There are a number of instances where professional help should always be sought. They include:

- Cases where symptoms like intrusive memories of the incident do not start to recede after a reasonable period
- Cases where victims become severely depressed and the depression does not appear to lift
- Cases where the victim is actively contemplating suicide
- Cases where normal human functions are seriously impaired

beyond a few days, e.g. sleeping, eating, sex
- Cases where the feelings that victims experience resurrect unresolved issues from previous (sometimes much earlier) trauma which is beyond the skill and experience of the helper concerned
- Cases where helpers involved feel they are getting out of their depth

All of these situations would merit seeking more professional help. However, it is important to recognize that professional support can be provided in two ways, e.g.:

- Firstly, by providing support and guidance for staff supporters/counsellors themselves, in order that they can continue working directly with more seriously affected victims (if carried out anonymously and does not involve further referral, this type of support need not involve the victim directly).
- Secondly, by providing a point for direct referral of victims themselves where they can receive more specialist help for ongoing or more serious reactions. Obviously this type of referral can only be carried out with the explicit agreement of the victim.

In large companies that employ or retain a professional counselling service both of these types of support will generally not be a problem. However, in companies where this option is not available the choices left open are the same as for smaller companies (discussed earlier in this chapter).

LIAISON WITH THE ORGANIZATION

In order for any form of follow-up or support service to be effective it must be able to offer complete confidentiality. Victims need to feel that whatever they disclose to a supporter or counsellor will not be related elsewhere or used against them in some way by the organization (or anyone else). Furthermore, regardless of whether anxieties about confidentiality are based on fact or fantasy, for many victims they exist, and as a consequence must be treated seriously. In other support or counselling settings this is not an issue. (For example, Victim Support, the Samaritans, etc., never reveal the names or details of any conversations with clients to anyone. Their work is entirely confidential as a matter of course.) However, one could argue that in commercial settings the situation is somewhat different.

In writing this section I recognize that for anyone who is involved with counselling in any way, this is a very sensitive issue. Nevertheless, it is one that cannot and should not be avoided when considering follow-up and support of victims at work. Perhaps, therefore, before leaping to conclusions, the best way forward is to consider the needs of all of the parties involved.

On the one hand victims need to be able to trust any counsellor or supporter who tries to help them recover from an experience. This is true whether help is offered in a one-to-one setting or through group de-briefing. For example, following an incident victims generally feel vulnerable and frightened that they have failed in some way. Furthermore, disclosing such feelings (particularly in a work setting) always seems risky. Yet disclosing feelings and talking about what they did, together with setting it into perspective, is the foundation of effective help. If, however, a victim suspects that any information they reveal will be related, recorded or used elsewhere, they will generally withdraw cooperation and the support service will quickly fall into disrepute. The need for confidentiality at this level cannot be overstated; it is central to effective support. Furthermore, where confidentiality is respected it will build trust and help make the whole initiative more effective.

On the other hand, however, few organizations will be prepared to resource a service that provides no information at all. It is the commercial equivalent of pouring money away (and will rarely be tolerated for long). Although I recognize and respect the counsellor's need for confidentiality, this has to be balanced against the organizational need to know that its money and resources are being used to good effect. As there are no general guidelines on this balancing act I can only draw on my own experience as a practitioner.

Generally I have found that senior managers in organizations are rarely interested in the detail of any work with victims (particularly when the need for confidentiality is explained rationally); their needs for information are more concerned with questions like:

- Is the service being used? (What are the gross numbers?)
- How much does it cost in terms of time and resources?
- Is it proving helpful? (Are we spending our money wisely?)
- Is there anything more we can or should be doing?

Usually organizational concerns are very genuine and are the result of very real concern for staff. Furthermore, satisfying requests for information at this level does not breach the level of confidentiality needed for working with victims. Indeed, I would even go so far as to suggest that any formal support service that is organized by a central coordinator would be well advised to provide general feedback to senior management on a regular basis (rather than waiting to be asked). However, having taken this step, it is vital that staff are told the 'ground rules' concerning confidentiality before they accept support, and should be encouraged to seek external help if this better meets their needs.

Where difficulty may arise is with individual cases. Generally concern about individual cases arises because they are exceptional in some way, e.g. cases involving long-term absence after an incident, or where an individual has a poor absence record prior to an incident and yet further absence afterwards, or where an individual is referred for external help which starts to prove expensive. One could reasonably argue that in all of these cases the organization has a legitimate interest in finding out more.

Although I would defend to the hilt the principle that counsellors/supporters should *never* divulge details of any case without the consent of the victim concerned, it may be possible to agree a satisfactory compromise. This will involve the counsellor talking with the victim to establish whether there are any areas of information that they would be prepared to disclose. In my own experience this has proved successful on many, many occasions. Generally cases of this type have a long history and the counsellor/ supporter will have been able to build up a very close relationship with the victim. As a consequence victims are nearly always more than happy to permit their counsellor to act as an advocate on their behalf.

As a final point I can only add that if the approach described above goes beyond a pure textbook definition of the role of a counsellor, then so be it. In my experience, by the time it becomes necessary to consider becoming an advocate, it is often desperately needed and always welcome.

THE ROLE OF THE SUPERVISOR AND/OR LINE MANAGER

In the days and weeks following an incident the immediate supervisor and/or line manager of a victim can play an important role in helping to facilitate their recovery. Even in companies that have a sophisticated professional support procedure, the day-to-day concern of immediate management is vital (and at least as highly valued by victims). Obviously formal support procedures are important, but they should not be seen to replace active local concern. However, before launching into a discussion of how supervisors and managers can demonstrate concern, try to complete the following exercise before reading any further.

Exercise 8.4
Imagine you are a manager and one of your team has been directly involved in a violent incident at work while you were out. You understand from the other team members that they were very badly shaken but not injured. After making a statement to the police they were taken home. From this point onwards, what action would you take?

As in previous exercises, record your thoughts on a separate sheet of paper so that you can compare them with the discussion that follows.

Active concern for victims can be demonstrated in many small but significant ways, e.g.:

- By making contact (either in person or by telephone) as soon as possible to find out how both they and their family are feeling/coping
- By supporting their requests for a graded re-entry back to work
- By gently encouraging and praising even small efforts to get back to normality
- By being available if needed
- By making opportunities from time to time to enquire genuinely how they are getting on (and listening to their reply). (Note that in this respect it is worth mentioning that there is a world of difference between asking a genuine question like, 'How are you?', as opposed to a loaded question like, 'You're alright now, aren't you?'. The genuine question seeks a genuine reply whereas the loaded question merely seeks confirmation that the victim is fine. This might seem obvious and a distinction not worth making, but I am amazed how often it happens.)
- By being sensitive to 'anniversaries' (e.g. same time of day and/or same day/week following an incident) and any other after-effects of an incident
- Where a victim takes sick-leave following an incident, making sure that telephone contact and/or home visits are arranged (particularly where any absence extends beyond a few days)

In many respects these actions simply add up to an active demonstration of human kindness. They are not soft or mollycoddling, and, even in today's competitive world, they can make a very significant difference in a victim's recovery. Indeed, I would even go so far as to say that they should be the automatic actions of any supervisor or manager once a member of their team has been confronted by trauma.

Finally, moving from the role of the line manager to more senior managerial groups, in the next section we will review a few other simple actions which can demonstrate active organizational concern.

OTHER HELPFUL ACTIONS

Although in themselves symbolic tokens, there are a few other lines of action which (when coupled with more comprehensive support structures) are often appreciated by victims, e.g.:

- Some organizations have made a custom of either sending victims a bouquet of flowers or, taking the entire group out for a meal together with their partners/spouses. At first sight both of these actions may seem somewhat trite; however, surprisingly, on balance they are appreciated by victims.
- Similarly, another form of action which is often appreciated is a letter from a senior manager or director expressing genuine concern about the employee's welfare.
- Another approach used in a few organizations is the equivalent of a 'royal visit'. In effect this is a visit by a senior manager, director or board member. Sadly, in large organizations, incidents have become so commonplace that this is no longer practical. However, it could still be worth considering in medium and smaller sized companies.

It is important to make sure that symbolic actions such as these are carried out genuinely. They are a bit like Americans using the phrase 'have a nice day'; unless said with genuine conviction, it sounds phoney and insincere. However, when it is expressed genuinely, it really can make a difference.

Finally, before closing this section it is also important to emphasize that, to be effective, symbolic actions must be used in conjunction with other more direct forms of acknowledgement and support. Indeed, if they are carried out in isolation they may well be viewed by staff as an insult. Equally, in some situations either approach must be used with caution. For example, where staff are subjected to multiple incidents then receiving a bunch of flowers every couple of months is hardly likely to be viewed charitably.

SUMMARY

- Follow-up and support can be broken into three main stages:
  - immediate post-incident emergency support
  - either individual follow-up or group de-briefing
  - longer term individual support
- Anyone involved in delivering an emergency response will need to know how to help people who are in shock.
- Using a 'standby team' to ensure a business gets back into operation quickly may appear commercially attractive, but needs to be used with caution.
- Several different approaches have been adopted for providing follow-up and support; they include:
  - using 'in-house' full-time professional counsellors to deal with all cases
  - using one or two full-time professional counsellors primarily as coordinators
  - extending the role of specialist staff, e.g. welfare or occupational health
  - using line managers, personnel or security staff
  - using an external consultant counsellor or counselling agency
- Victims in smaller organizations will generally need to seek support in the wider community.
- Proactively offering follow-up and support should become a normal everyday action after an incident has taken place. It should provide confidential emotional support, practical help and appropriate information.
- Support procedures which are used to help victims of violence and crime at work can be useful for helping victims of other types of trauma.

- Some people will need longer term support, e.g. victims who have been very seriously affected or victims (or witnesses) who become involved with police or judicial procedures.
- Non-professionals who become involved with helping victims will need to understand when to seek professional help.
- Although providing general feedback to the organization is important, it should never disclose details of individual cases without the explicit prior agreement of the victims concerned.
- Even where a company uses a sophisticated professional support procedure it should not replace day-to-day concern by the supervisor or immediate line manager.
- Symbolic tokens can be useful additional forms of help, but only where they are used in conjunction with more direct forms of support.

9

Implications for training

WHAT ARE THE IMPLICATIONS FOR TRAINING?

No doubt by now you will have recognized that any serious effort to address violence and crime at work will have considerable implications for training. However, before discussing these in detail, it could be worth taking a few minutes to complete the following exercise.

Exercise 9.1
Thinking about your own particular organization (and what you have read in the previous chapters), what specific training initiatives could help address violence and crime where you work? In addressing this question it might help if you consider:

- *Staff who could be directly involved either as victims or witnesses*
- *Supervisors and managers of staff who are in the 'front line' of any incident*
- *Other specialists (such as personnel, welfare or occupational health) who may become involved at some stage*
- *Other staff who may become involved in a supporting role, either within the first few hours or in the days and weeks that follow*

Alternatively, if your company already offers training and/or support for anyone who is involved in an incident at work, you may find it more useful to consider:

- *What your company does now*
- *The effectiveness of any action (both for staff who are directly involved and others who may become involved later on)*
- *What could be done to develop and improve the service your company offers*

As before, record your thoughts on a separate sheet of paper so that you can compare them with the ideas presented in the rest of this chapter.

The extent of any training concerned with violence and crime at work will depend on the amount of investment that an organization is prepared to devote to this type of work. Clearly, this will be heavily influenced by the size and scale of the problem and the particular organizational circumstances. Hence there is a need to monitor the scale of incidents before doing anything.

However, assuming there is a problem, then the range of training options that could be pursued is very wide and no doubt choices will have to be made about where to start. Indeed, training could include a whole variety of different types of events depending on how far a company is prepared to become involved, e.g.:

- Training for staff who may be directly involved in an incident could include:
  - specific training on how to minimize and manage aggression and abuse
  - general training on how to respond in the event of a violent incident
  - specific training on the support available and self-help skills in the event of being involved in an incident
- Training for managers and supervisors of staff who are employed in high-risk, 'front-line' occupations could include:
  - general awareness training on the impact of violence and crime together with highlighting the supervisor's or manager's role following an incident
  - simple support skills to help staff recover
- Training for more senior managers or other professional groups who become involved with victims during the first few hours after an incident could include:
  - simple support skills together with specific training for helping staff who are in shock
- Training for other staff who become involved with victims as

part of a more formal support network (e.g. peer counsellors), as a minimum, must include:
— more extensive training in support skills
— guidance about the 'normal' range of reactions that victims are likely to experience
— guidance on when to seek further help

Subsequent sections of this chapter will look in more detail at each of these types of training. For the benefit of readers who are not from a training background, I will also outline specific training objectives for each type of training. These will be cross-referenced to earlier chapters where information can be found for the content of the training. Furthermore, illustration training designs will be included in Appendix 2. However, in order to be effective, training will need to be delivered by staff who are skilled at running training events. This could be either training specialists or managers, supervisors or other specialist staff who are skilled in delivering occasional training.

Finally, it is important to point out that whatever training a company chooses to carry out, it cannot be a 'once and for all' effort. Refresher training will also be needed from time to time to ensure that skills and knowledge are kept up to date.

TRAINING FOR STAFF WHO MAY BE DIRECTLY INVOLVED IN AN INCIDENT

As we have seen in the previous section, training for staff who may be directly involved in an incident can be addressed at up to three levels, depending on a company's needs. These are:

• Specific training on how to manage and minimize aggression and abuse
• General training on how to respond in the event of an incident
• Specific training on the support available and self-help skills in the event of being involved in an incident

From a commercial point of view it makes a great deal of sense to examine these types of training very carefully. They are about preparing staff in the event of an incident, equipping them with the skills to cope at the time and providing them with knowledge and skills to help themselves afterwards. This will help to minimize the psychological impact of incidents and speed up recovery afterwards. For the organization this translates directly into minimizing any losses. Furthermore, all of these topics may be very real concerns for staff who perceive themselves to be in 'high-risk' situations.

At the outset, it is important to stress that addressing staff concerns need not involve long and involved training sessions. Often they can be highlighted and addressed within a company's existing training framework. For example, sessions on all three topics could be included during induction training for new entrants, or as part of normal ongoing training. Indeed, there is a strong case for not presenting this kind of training as anything special. To do so could well heighten staff concerns and unnecessarily increase anxiety levels. Although violence and crime is increasingly common in the workplace, it is important to keep it in perspective; most people we meet at work do not become abusive or violent and even fewer are motivated by criminal intent.

Nevertheless, this should not be used as an excuse for 'sweeping the problem under the carpet'. Staff concerns need to be addressed and addressed seriously. It is therefore important to look in a little more detail at what each of the three types of training could involve.

Training to manage and minimize aggression and abuse

In many organizations this is probably the greatest area of training need. Practically every survey that has been carried out confirms that aggression and abuse are by far the most prevalent types of incident at work. In terms of training objectives, if staff are to manage and minimize aggression and abuse they need to be able to:

- Identify and appreciate the different types of situations or circumstances that can lead to frustration and anger.
- Take action (as far as they are able) to change any physical causes of frustration (e.g. in shops and offices, taking action to minimize queuing or wasting people's time).
- Identify the early warning signs that someone is becoming potentially aggressive.
- Adapt their behaviour to 'defuse' frustrating or aggressive situations before they erupt into overt violence.

These objectives can be met in a variety of ways from a series of half-hour bursts (as part of normal office/shop training) through to a one or two day dedicated training programme. The basic information required for such training has already been discussed in Chapter 5 in the sections dealing with 'prevention measures' and 'managing aggression and abuse'. However, turning this information into effective and interesting training means more than just providing lectures or presentations. It also means designing relevant exercises so that staff can apply the ideas to their own working situation, e.g.:

- Invite staff to work in small groups to 'brainstorm' what causes people to become frustrated, angry or abusive in their workplace.
- Hold a group discussion or action planning session for staff to work out what they can do to modify or remove aspects of their working environment that incite frustration and aggression.
- Use simulation and/or practical exercises to help staff identify the early warning signs that indicate that someone is becoming increasingly frustrated or angry.
- Use realistic role-play to help staff practice skills in 'defusing' people who are aggressive or abusive.

Two alternative designs which illustrate how all of these points can be brought together can be found in Examples 1 and 2 in Appendix 2.

Training on how to respond in the event of a violent incident

Although violent incidents are far less common than incidents involving aggression and abuse, in many organizations they still pose a high risk for front-line staff. Where this is the case, training in how to respond should be a high priority. In terms of training objectives this means that staff should be able to:

- Respond in a way that minimizes danger to themselves or others and, at the same time, minimizes any loss to the company.
- Operate any security equipment (e.g. alarms, cameras, etc.).
- Implement personal strategies that help to minimize the psychological impact of an incident.
- Implement organizational policy with regard to post-incident procedures.

The basic information underpinning these objectives can be found in Chapter 7 in the sections 'appropriate organizational procedures' and 'helping staff develop personal coping strategies'. Beyond this, a few ideas for exercises to help staff consolidate this information could include:

- (Assuming an incident procedure exists) using workplace-based practical exercises and/or simulation to 'dry-run' the procedure in absolute safety. However, it is important to remember that these exercises will need to be repeated several times to ensure that staff can respond automatically.
- Exercises to help staff visualize what they would think and do in the event of an incident. In particular helping them develop their own personal coping strategies.
- An exercise to help staff develop their powers of observation for noting important features which may help identify any assailant.
- Simulation exercises to rehearse how to implement an immediate post-incident response.

As this type of training is highly workplace specific, it is generally most effective when carried out in the normal working environment. Staff need to be able to carry out all of the incident procedures in their normal workplace. It therefore follows that an off-the-job training room can rarely simulate this effectively. Generally this also means that training will need to be integrated into the normal workplace training framework.

Training in self-help skills and how to access support in the aftermath of an incident

Staff who are aware of the effects of violent incidents (and what to do to help themselves) will, as a general rule, recover more quickly than staff who are not aware. Although paradoxical, it follows that training before an incident is an important aid for recovery afterwards. The main objectives which this type of training needs to address involves equipping staff with knowledge and skills so that they are able to:

● Recognize both the common effects of violent incidents and when to seek further help.
● Practise simple self-help skills that aid recovery.
● Obtain access to further support, either internally within the company or externally from the wider community.

Once again, most of the basic information needed to support these objectives can be found in Chapter 6, 'the effects of violence and crime on individuals', Chapter 7, in the section 'other self-help techniques', and Chapter 8, 'follow-up and support'. Activities to support this information could include:

● A group exercise for staff to think about how they envisage they might react in the hours and days following an incident (or how they actually reacted if they have ever been involved in an incident or other form of trauma)
● Exercises to practise self-help skills (e.g. relaxation, listening and simple personal support skills)

Although for the purpose of discussion, this particular aspect of training has been separated from the previous section (how to respond at the time of an incident), clearly they are directly linked. In practice, therefore, the two topics are probably best coupled together. An illustration of this combination can be found in Example 3 in Appendix 2.

Finally, before moving on to consider training for other groups, it is important to add a note of caution. Any training that requires staff to think about incidents at work (whether overtly violent or not) can resurrect unresolved issues for anyone who has actually been involved in an incident. As a result they may become upset and require individual help. Obviously training should not set out with the intent of upsetting participants. However, the nature of the subject is such that, sooner or later, it could strike a raw nerve. This in turn has implications for the skill of trainers who deliver such events; i.e. they need to be competent both in delivering training and, where necessary, providing personal support.

TRAINING FOR MANAGERS AND SUPERVISORS OF STAFF WHO ARE AT RISK

The section 'the role of the supervisor and/or line manager' (in Chapter 8) pointed out how small thoughtful actions by managers and supervisors can facilitate the rate at which a victim recovers from an incident. Although the skills involved are based on simple common sense, it is surprising how often they are ignored. Even the most considerate of managers sometimes may be paralysed if a member of their team is involved in an incident. Furthermore, the source of their inaction is often rooted in fear that something they say or do will make the victim's condition even worse. As a result they may do nothing. I can only repeat what was stated earlier (see Chapter 8, p. 139), 'The only way anyone from a victim's workplace can exacerbate [a victim's] condition is by trivializing or discounting their experience.'

Although common sense, training that raises awareness and highlights these skills simply gives permission for them to be used.

Often there is little that managers or supervisors need to learn which is new; training merely prompts action and reinforces helpful behaviour. However, for victims this can make all the difference.

It is also important to emphasize that the training involved with this group need not involve extensive or time consuming off-the-job courses. It can be satisfactorily addressed through well designed intensive training inputs added on to normal management meetings. The actual training design needs to be thought through and planned in just as much detail as for any other type of training. Starting with the training objectives, these could include enabling managers and supervisors to:

- Recognize the extent of violence and crime within their own organization.
- Act with confidence when helping victims following an incident.
- Carry out a range of basic personal support skills.
- Recognize when a member of staff needs to be referred for more professional help.

The basic information which underpins these objectives can be found generally in Chapters 2 and 3 together with Chapter 8, in the sections 'the role of the supervisor and/or line manager' and 'when to seek professional help'. For further discussion of the actual techniques for providing personal support the reader is directed to the publications listed in Appendix 3. Skills and techniques for providing personal support have been discussed at length by many other authors and therefore they will not be repeated here.

However, a few ideas for exercises and activities to support the objectives could include:

- A focused group discussion to identify ideas and actions that have proved helpful with victims in the past (or in other settings)
- Simulation/role-play exercises in pairs (or trios) to develop

and extend personal support skills

- A group exercise (with guidance if needed) to identify a checklist of indicators for when more professional help is needed

Precisely how these ideas can be combined in practice is illustrated in Example 4 in Appendix 2.

TRAINING FOR STAFF WHO BECOME INVOLVED WITH VICTIMS DURING THE FIRST FEW HOURS AFTER AN INCIDENT

As we have seen from earlier chapters, during the first few hours after an incident victims (and witnesses) are often in a state of shock. It follows, therefore, that anyone (senior manager, security officer, personnel, occupational health or welfare officer) who makes contact with victims during this time will need to be versed in how to help people who are in shock. Furthermore, it is important not to underestimate the anxiety this role can create for anyone who has to carry it out. Without training, even professional staff often feel inadequate and ill-equipped to cope with the demands placed upon them. Typically they do not have a yardstick (other than their intuition) to measure whether their actions help or hinder.

This is where training can be of enormous help. As a minimum the objectives of such training would ensure that participants are able to:

- Recognize typical behavioural symptoms when people are in shock.
- Carry out appropriate action to help defuse shock reactions.
- Offer information and practical help where needed.
- Recognize when to call for more professional support.

Once again the basic information which underpins these objectives can be found in earlier chapters, i.e. Chapter 6, 'immediate effects of an incident', and Chapter 8, 'post-incident emergency support' and 'when to seek professional help'. Ideas for activities and exercises could include:

- A focused group discussion to identify (and record) typical shock reactions to traumatic situations
- A brainstorming activity to identify actions which help to defuse shock
- Simulation/role-play to develop and extend defusing skills
- A group discussion to identify what types of practical help may be needed after an incident
- A group exercise (with guidance if needed) to identify instances where more professional help may be needed

An illustration of a training design which utilizes these ideas can be found in Example 5 in Appendix 2.

TRAINING FOR STAFF WHO MAY BECOME INVOLVED WITH VICTIMS ON A MORE FORMAL BASIS

Whereas the other types of training discussed so far are fairly short (and if necessary can be delivered without making lengthy separate arrangements), training for staff who become involved with victims as part of a more formal support network is different. Often it will be carried out in an off-the-job setting, initially involving anything from 1 to 5 days of intensive training (depending on the objectives to be achieved, who is involved and their level of prior experience, and the resources a company is prepared to invest).

Depending on the approach chosen by a company (which may be dictated by size and staff available), employees who may be trained to support victims could be drawn from:

- Line managers and/or supervisors
- Existing specialist staff (e.g. personnel, security, occupational health or welfare)
- Ordinary members of staff (usually volunteers)

Clearly, the training needs of each of these groups may vary and this would need to be reflected in the actual training design. However, before launching into the detail of any training it is important to add a word of caution. One or two of the people who volunteer (or are nominated) to provide support for victims may sometimes be victims themselves who are still deeply affected by their own memories. It is as if they seek to exorcise their own pain through helping others. In itself being a victim should never exclude anyone from providing help. Indeed, a volunteer (or nominee) who has lived through and recovered from an incident can often demonstrate far greater sensitivity and understanding for other victims than anyone who does not have first-hand experience of an incident. However, problems arise where a volunteer's own pain is so overwhelming that it interferes with their ability to listen and provide effective help. Furthermore, this is often not picked up during the selection of volunteers/nominees and only becomes evident during training (as the following case study illustrates).

Case Study 9.1

Bill had been employed as an area personnel officer with a large national security firm for about four years. In response to the rising number of violent incidents involving staff, the company decided to provide a support service involving all area personnel officers. As soon as Bill heard about the proposal he became one of its greatest advocates, saying it should have been provided years ago.

A three day training programme was arranged and Bill joined the first group to attend. By lunch-time on the first day it was obvious to everyone on the programme that Bill had experienced a serious incident which was still at the forefront of his mind. Throughout the morning, whenever an opportunity arose he more or less took over the session, talking in an agitated way about what he knew people went through after an incident. Furthermore, it was clear from the way he spoke that he was relating his own personal experience.

During the lunch break one of the trainers took the opportunity to talk with Bill privately. It emerged that some seven years earlier he had been the victim of a savage assault one evening, sustaining severe physical injuries. Furthermore, it was also evident that much though his physical wounds had healed long ago, the psychological damage had not. He still suffered from periods of insomnia together with flashback memories of the incident. To the dismay of his family, since then he tried to avoid going out on an evening and had stopped watching many television programmes and news reports for fear they would trigger another attack of sleeplessness.

For the sake of brevity, suffice it to say that towards the end of the discussion Bill began to recognize that rather than becoming involved with the support network, his more immediate need was to find help with his own suffering.

In my experience, Bill's case is not exceptional. Although not an everyday occurrence, it is not unusual to find people who are in need of help themselves joining (or being nominated for) a training programme to support others. This raises two important issues which are directly relevant for this type of training:

- Firstly, it highlights the sensitive issue of whether training should be used as part of the selection procedure for members of a support group. In my own view this is entirely appropriate; training can contribute to selection in three important ways:
  - by identifying volunteers/nominees (like Bill) who need help themselves before they are able to offer help to others.
  - by identifying nominees who either do not want to be involved or feel really ill-at-ease carrying out such a role.
  - by identifying any volunteer/nominee who simply does not develop an adequate repertoire of skills to be able to offer real help to victims.

  Provided the training input to selection is carried out with sensitivity by the trainer(s), it can make an additional useful contribution to the selection process as a whole. However, this must be carried out openly; trainees need to be aware of both the selection procedure and the role played by training. (Note that it is also important to add that where an individual does not complete the training (or completes the training but decides not to practise actual support activity), the organization must be prepared to accept the decision without prejudice to the individual concerned. Furthermore, the possibility of this happening must be carefully negotiated and agreed with appropriate people in the organization *before* any training is even started.)

- Secondly, it highlights important areas of skill for any trainer who is involved in this kind of work; i.e. they must be able to offer a high level of personal support to participants if the occasion demands. Furthermore, they must also have easy access to other more professional help if needed.

Having added these words of caution we can turn once again to the specific training objectives. Clearly the number of objectives that can be achieved will be restricted by the time available for training. However, by way of illustration, they could include the following, which ensure that by the end of the training participants are able to:

- Offer effective support both to victims and their immediate families (if needed).
- Respond appropriately to feelings and emotions expressed by victims.
- Recognize and facilitate 'normal' patterns of recovery.
- Provide appropriate guidance, information and advice (as needed).
- Identify when more professional help may be needed and, as a consequence, respond appropriately.
- Recognize the boundaries of a supporter's role in respect of organizational constraints.
- Where appropriate (and agreed with the victim), liaise with other individuals or groups within the organization.
- Recognize when to seek help themselves either to meet their own needs or the needs of a victim.
- Make constructive use of arrangements for supervision and support.

Although some of these objectives are similar to the objectives specified for other groups, they are profoundly different. The difference lies in the depth and scope of skills and knowledge which members of a support network need to be able to demonstrate. If a support network is to be credible, then network members need to be able to provide a level of support over and above that provided elsewhere within the company. Furthermore, it is important to emphasize 'over and above'. The existence of a support network must be in addition to the day-to-day help provided by other staff. Where it is used instead of day-to-day support then the results will often be highly dysfunctional (probably undermining the whole initiative).

However, to return to the main theme, in common with earlier sections, the basic information that underpins these objectives can be found throughout Chapter 6, the section 'other self-help techniques' in Chapter 7, various sections of Chapter 8 and Appendix 4, 'supervision and support of staff supporters'. For details of the techniques and skills for providing personal support the reader is directed to Appendix 3, which lists other useful publications.

Finally, a few ideas for exercises and activities to support the training objectives could include:

- Extensive simulation/role-play exercises based on highly realistic or actual incidents (assuming the actual victims involved have given their permission) which participants could encounter during their support work. Ideally these would involve using video recordings of the exercises for personal feedback and skill building. A further option which adds even more realism could include using actors to simulate the victim roles.
- Using realistic case studies or (where permission is given) case histories. These can be used in a variety of ways, e.g. to help participants identify:
  - appropriate skills or actions needed
  - who else might need to be involved (either inside or outside the organization)
  - when to request more professional help

- A 'socio-drama' type of activity to examine how the aftermath of an incident affects the relationships between a victim, their colleagues at work and family and friends. (Note that this type of activity will require a highly skilled facilitator to ensure that it is used to best effect.)
- Providing personal interview time with the trainer(s) (on an individual basis) to help clarify how each participant feels about both the programme and the prospect of being involved with supporting victims.
- Structured group exercises to establish and examine:
  − boundaries of the supporters role (both in terms of work with victims and organizational constraints)
  − what other sources of help are available, both internally within the company and externally in the wider community
  − lines of communication with other relevant individuals or groups in the organization
- Various exercises to explore:
  − dealing with feelings and emotions effectively
  − how to facilitate recovery effectively
  − factors which may complicate a victim's recovery

As there are wide variations in the actual design of training for staff involved in more formal support, two illustrations are given in Appendix 2 (i.e. Examples 6 and 7). Example 6 outlines a highly effective one day programme designed by the Victim Support 'Crime at Work' Training Team, whereas Example 7 gives details of a more extensive three day residential design.

KEEPING UP TO DATE

Once any initial training has been completed, it is vital that the skills and knowledge that staff have acquired are kept up to date. This implies designing some form of ongoing refresher training which can be delivered from time to time. Although the idea of ongoing training was mentioned in Chapter 7, it will be pursued in more detail here. In some respects it is also fair to add that designing and implementing ongoing training is even more challenging than designing initial training. Inevitably it presents a number of significant issues. With respect to staff who may be directly involved in an incident (and their supervisors and immediate managers), these include:

- How to keep ongoing training fresh, interesting and alive
- How to deal with geographical variations in incidents (and, therefore, the effect this has on the need for ongoing training)
- How to ensure that any training causes minimum disruption to normal working patterns
- How to ensure that staff stay adequately alert but not unnecessarily anxious

Each of these points will be taken in turn.

Keeping ongoing training fresh, interesting and alive

In some organizations staff sit down ritually every 3 to 6 months during a staff training session and read through the incident procedure. While this may be better than doing nothing at all, it is not a very good way of holding their interest. By way of contrast, more creative options could include:

- Assuming they exist and are available in the company, different specialists who may be able to provide a useful input should be involved (e.g. personnel, security, occupational health, members of the peer support network, etc.).
- A 'trivial pursuits' type of quiz could be held on procedures for responding to incidents.
- A discussion and review of particular aspects of responding to incidents that have proved problematic could be organized.
- A 'What would you do if . . .?' exercise could be organized where staff prepare the scenarios themselves from their own experience before the training session starts (as a form of pre-work).

All of these options are far more likely to engage the interest of staff and prevent the topic becoming boring and stale.

Geographical variations in incidents

As was pointed out in Chapter 7, current geographical trends in incidents mean that staff who work in London and the South East are far more likely to be using incident procedures for real than elsewhere in the country. This poses a real dilemma for any ongoing training. Effectively it means that staff in high-risk areas may be highly experienced at responding to incidents whereas staff in lower risk areas may have little or no experience at all (other than that gained through simulation exercises).

This has direct implications for training. In situations where incidents occur on a fairly regular basis (i.e. recurrent serious incidents once or twice a year), there is a greater need for incident reviews than there is for specific refresher training. However, in situations where incidents are less frequent, the need to be prepared can only be reinforced effectively through ongoing training.

Minimizing disruption to normal working

In effect minimizing disruption to normal working usually means 'fitting in' with normal working patterns. Nowadays this should be less of a problem than was the case several years ago. In many organizations the need for ongoing training and/or regular staff communication is widely recognized. Brief but regular staff training sessions, team briefing and/or quality circle meetings often form part of normal organizational life. All of these settings can be used for ongoing training which makes a real contribution to the organization. Furthermore, they offer the added bonus of creating no further disruption to normal working than that which exists already.

Maximizing effectiveness without creating undue anxiety

Maximizing the effectiveness of ongoing training without generating undue anxiety for staff generally raises two concerns: firstly, the frequency of events and, secondly, the content and style in which they are carried out. Chapter 7 advocated approximately 6 monthly intervals as probably an appropriate time-scale between ongoing events. However, of equal importance is the content and style of delivery. Anxiety among staff can be minimized (without compromising effectiveness) through training sessions which present a truthful picture of the risks involved but at the same time focus on effective coping and response strategies. Although it may be tempting to concentrate on the more traumatic events (as these tend to be more memorable), they constitute less than 1 per cent of incidents as a whole and do not give a representative picture. By contrast, presenting a more honest picture not only gives a more balanced perspective but also minimizes undue anxiety. Similarly, the style of delivery need not be onerous and foreboding. Indeed, training can generally be more effective when presented in a way that is interesting and stimulating, perhaps using some of the ideas discussed earlier.

We turn next to ongoing training for staff who are involved with victims during the first few hours after an incident. The prime need for this group will be some form of regular review meeting (i.e. every 6 months or so depending on the frequency of incidents) where they can share experiences and discuss any anxieties or difficulties. As the number of staff involved is likely to be quite small, generally it is unrealistic to design separate arrangements for those who are regularly involved with victims and those who are not. Review meetings will usually satisfy the needs of both. Providing an opportunity for staff who have been involved with victims to examine their actions will also help staff who have had little or no involvement to review their own skills and learn from the experience of other colleagues.

Last but not least, the ongoing training needs of more formal support staff must be addressed. This can be tackled in at least two ways:

- Through supervision and support with individual casework
- Through ongoing/further training and development

Supervision and support of staff who work with victims is essential and is discussed in Appendix 4. However, as a separate issue, ongoing training is also important in order to develop and extend the skills of members of the support network. Furthermore, in large organizations where individual staff supporters are spread over a wide geographical area, training can also help to weld them into a more cohesive team. The types of issues and topics that could be addressed include:

- Consolidation and extension of existing skills
- Specific new skills to deal with particular problems that may affect victims, e.g.:
  - helping with insomnia
  - anxiety management
  - managing the return to normal working
  - addressing the needs of a victim's family
  - etc.
- Dealing with difficulties and problems
- Other relaxation techniques
- etc.

It is inevitable that initial training will only cover elementary aspects of providing personal support. Nowadays there is a vast reservoir of additional subjects and skills which could provide valuable source materials for this type of ongoing training. Indeed, it is often the case that having undergone initial training some members of the support group become so enthusiastic they carry on (outside any organizational provision) to gain more formal qualifications in counselling and support.

SUMMARY

- Serious efforts to address violence and crime at work will inevitably have significant training implications.
- A range of training options may be possible; they could include:
  - training for staff who may be directly involved in an incident

- training for supervisors and managers of staff who are at risk
- training for other staff who become involved with victims during the first few hours after an incident
- training for staff who become involved with victims as part of a more formal support network

- Training for staff who may be directly involved in an incident could address:
  - helping them minimize aggression and abuse
  - what to do in the event of a serious incident
  - self-help skills coupled with how to access personal support
- Training for managers and supervisors of staff in high-risk settings primarily concerns:
  - the role of the manager/supervisor
  - simple support skills to help staff recover
- Training for other staff who become involved with victims during the first few hours after an incident is primarily about how to help people who are in shock.
- As a minimum, training staff who are involved with a more formal support structure concerns:
  - more extensive training in personal support skills
  - guidance on the normal range of reactions that victims may experience
  - guidance on when to seek more professional help
- Once any initial training has been completed, it is vital that skills and knowledge are kept up to date, through incident reviews and/or periodic refresher training.

10

Developing a comprehensive strategy for action

INTRODUCTION

No doubt by now it will have become clear that there is no single ideal solution which an organization can adopt to deal with violence and crime at work. It depends on a whole variety of factors, e.g.:

- The size of the organization. As we have seen, these vary from the corner shop all the way through to large plcs and multi-nationals.
- The resources available.
- The geographical spread of the organization, e.g. single locations through to hundreds of offices, shops or outlets spread across the entire country (and in some cases in other countries as well).
- The organization and management structure.
- Whether specialist departments such as welfare, occupational health, security or personnel even exist in a particular company.
- The types of employees affected, e.g. office and shop workers through to staff who carry out individual delivery or service work in a vast array of different settings.
- The types of incidents experienced.

All of these factors conspire to make it impossible to recommend any one approach over and above any other. Nevertheless, despite this it should be possible to pull together all of the different strands outlined in the earlier chapters into a cohesive strategy for action. This will be the task here.

At the outset, however, it is important to emphasize once again that taking action on violence and crime at work does not come about because of a 'knee-jerk' reaction to a particular incident. All too often 'doing something' about violence and crime is triggered by a particularly horrific incident where both staff and management panic and run round in circles not knowing what to do for the best. Generally the action that follows is haphazard, piecemeal and of little long-term help. Borrowing an expression first used by Jones,[18] developing an appropriate framework for providing effective help means:

> Getting it right
> Doing it well,
> and
> Making it stick.

This cannot be emphasized too much; sound policy for dealing with incidents is essential. Senior management must demonstrate real commitment to tackling the issue. The Health and Safety Executive outline a simple approach to tackling violence and crime in their pamphlet 'Violence to staff'[4] and in their Guidance Notes for the financial sector. However, the section that follows provides further detail and distinguishes between action which is aimed at tackling aggression and abuse and action to tackle overt violence and crime.

A STRATEGY FOR COMPREHENSIVE ACTION

Step 1. Identify an individual (or group) who will take responsibility for researching the problem and recommending appropriate action
Clearly, when an organization chooses to address violence and crime, some individual or group has to be prepared to carry out the spadework. In small organizations the choice may be self-evident; however, in larger companies several different people (or specialist groups) may have an interest. Deciding who is most appropriate involves considering a number of key questions:

- Who has a known interest in the topic?
- Does anyone have current or previous experience of addressing violence and crime at work?
- Who is most likely to engender the trust of staff in order to establish their views?

Step 2. Establish the scope of seriousness of the problem
Given that an individual or coordinating group has been identified, the next essential step is to establish the size and seriousness of the problem. As was pointed out in Chapter 4, generally this means asking the staff who are likely to be directly involved. In order to do this effectively three key issues will need to be considered:

- Who to ask—all staff or a representative sample?
- What questions to ask? As we saw in Chapter 4, this could affect the scope of incidents considered worth reporting.
- What mechanism to use for asking? Options available include questionnaires, using individual face-to-face interviews, using existing meetings, ongoing training sessions or dedicated group meetings.

Full details of all of the points to be considered when carrying out a staff survey are given in Chapter 4.

Step 3. Establish a regular monitoring procedure
Once the initial survey has been carried out (assuming it reveals there is a problem worth addressing further), the next step usually involves setting up a regular monitoring procedure to ensure that all incidents are reported on a regular basis. This provides the basic management information on which any further decisions can be made. Once again, full details of how to set about establishing a procedure are given in Chapter 4.

Step 4. Review information and decide what types of incidents to tackle
Armed with the survey results and any information flowing from the monitoring procedure, the coordinator (or group) should be in a position to decide (or make recommendations) on the type of incidents worth tackling. For reasons of simplicity (and following the main thrust of this text) I would suggest two broad categories: 'aggression and abuse' and 'violence and crime'. However, if the results from the survey and regular monitoring suggest other more appropriate categories, there is no reason why they should not be included as well.

However, assuming the two categories ('abuse and aggression' and 'violence and crime') are appropriate, the steps which follow for each are significantly different (see Fig. 10.1 for further clarification on this point). Obviously, it is possible to work on both categories at once, but usually it makes more sense to concentrate on one at a time. In the text that follows 'aggression and abuse' will be addressed first and 'violence and crime' second.

Subsequent sequence of actions to tackle aggression and abuse

Step 5. Review information on typical situations where incidents occur
Having decided to tackle aggression and abuse, it is vital that any actions directly address the types of incident that staff encounter in their day-to-day work. This implies reviewing all of the

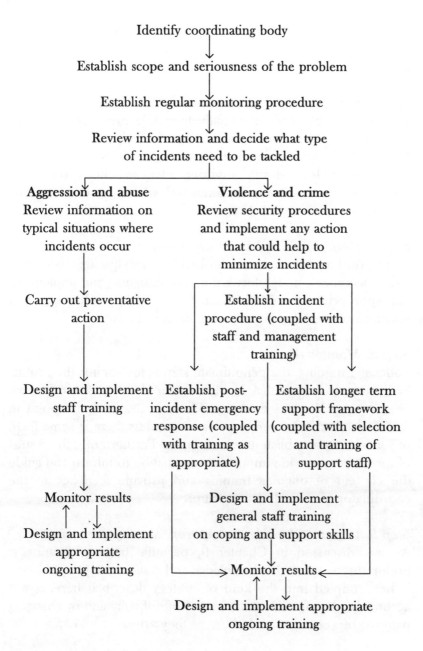

Figure 10.1   A strategy for comprehensive action—flow chart

information gathered about aggressive and abusive incidents in order to establish which are most common and require priority attention.

Step 6. Carry out preventative action
Chapter 5 highlighted how relatively simple preventative actions such as changing the workplace layout can help to prevent many potentially aggressive incidents arising at all. It makes sense, therefore, before doing anything else to check out what preventative measures can be taken and, where possible, ensuring they are carried out (see Chapter 5 for further details).

Step 7. Design and implement staff training
Once priorities have been established then tackling aggression and abuse becomes a straightforward task of designing and implementing appropriate training. Chapter 9 and Appendix 2 give a selection of ideas for how this can be carried out.

Step 8. Monitor results
Following training, the penultimate step is to monitor the results. Sadly this is a step that is often ignored or tagged on as an afterthought. Yet it is essential. There is absolutely no point in investing valuable resources in training unless there is some form of follow-up to establish its effectiveness. Furthermore, the results of monitoring provide important information to inform and guide the content of ongoing training and provide feedback to the coordinator (or coordinating group).

Step 9. Design and implement appropriate ongoing training
As was discussed in Chapter 9, periodic ongoing training is important to ensure that knowledge and skills are kept up to date. When coupled into the kind of strategy described here, it will accurately identify and address areas of difficulty and/or changing patterns of aggression and abuse as they arise.

Subsequent sequence of actions to tackle violence and crime

Step 5. Review security procedures and implement any action that could help to minimize incidents

Although this is a topic that has not been mentioned in previous chapters, it is an obvious next step. The reason for the omission is because of the size and scope of the topic. Security is a specialist subject in its own right and requires serious attention, which is beyond the scope of this text. Therefore, rather than offering superficial suggestions here, the reader would be better advised to approach a security specialist for information and advice.

Obviously it makes sense to try to keep incidents to a minimum. However, it is important to add that there is no simple link between the level of security provided and occurrence of incidents. Even premises that are highly protected with sophisticated security systems are still subject to crime and violence. Indeed, some aggressors seem to treat security measures with disdain, e.g. robbers who deliberately smile and pose for video cameras (yes, it does happen)!

Step 6. Establish an incident procedure

Having chosen to tackle violence and crime, the next essential step is to establish an incident procedure appropriate to the circumstances in which incidents take place. Clearly, the steps involved will differ from one work setting to another. For example, an appropriate procedure for staff who work on delivery duties will be very different to the procedure for staff who work in a high street retail shop or office. The points that need to be considered when developing (or reviewing) an incident procedure are fully discussed in Chapter 7.

Finally, having developed an appropriate procedure, staff will need to be informed and trained on what it involves and what they are required to do.

Step 7. Preamble

When addressing violence and crime, step 7 can involve up to three avenues for parallel action. Although they are all of equal importance (and therefore could be carried out at the same time— resources permitting), in most settings a decision will be required concerning which to work on first. It is therefore important to emphasize that the sequence that follows is purely the author's own preference. Tackling each of the three routes for action in a different sequence is equally acceptable.

Step 7a. Establish a post-incident emergency response
Chapter 8 pointed out that an effective post-incident response provides immediate help and support for staff who are affected by an incident, and at the same time ensures that the organization gets back into normal operation as soon as practicable. However, it is also worth pointing out that staff who work in companies that carry out an emergency response always appreciate this kind of help. Indeed, in many instances it is often perceived as one of the most important aspects of victim support.

General guidelines on the points to be considered when developing a response procedure are discussed in detail in Chapter 8, while Chapter 9 and Appendix 2 provide guidelines for developing appropriate training for staff who carry out this type of work.

Step 7b. Establish a longer term support framework
Although immediate post-incident support is important, it should not detract from longer term help. In particular this means providing either individual or group de-briefing and, where necessary, much longer term help with victims who are seriously affected and with anyone involved with police or judicial processes.

It is also worth noting that this step, probably more than any other, offers a wide range of different options on how to provide support. As we saw in Chapter 8, this can range from providing a specialist professional counselling service through to developing a group of volunteers (or nominated) supporters drawn from staff, management or other specialist departments. However, perhaps the key point to emphasize here is that whatever approach is chosen, any volunteer (or nominated) supporters will require additional training in order to carry out the role effectively. Details of all of the points that need to be considered both for establishing a support framework and training of any staff involved are given in Chapters 8 and 9 and Appendix 2.

Step 7c. Design and implement general staff training on coping and support skills
Whereas both other forms of action in step 7 are about post-incident responses, this step seeks, firstly, to provide help during an incident (through coping techniques) and, secondly, to ensure an adequate level of day-to-day support afterwards. Once again both of these actions are of fundamental importance. Coping techniques will help to minimize the impact of an incident, while support from colleagues and local management provides help on a day-to-day basis. Indeed, it is worth remembering that where support at a local level is absent for some reason then the effectiveness of the whole initiative will be seriously undermined. Details of all of these points can be found in various sections throughout Chapters 7, 8 and 9 and Appendix 2.

Step 8. Monitor results
As with the earlier discussion concerning training to minimize and manage aggression and abuse, monitoring the results of all of the actions in step 7 is vital. Once again, not only will it provide information on the effectiveness of training but will also serve to guide and focus any further effort.

Step 9. Design and implement appropriate ongoing training
Finally, appropriate ongoing training is the key to making sure that the skills and knowledge of everyone involved or concerned with violence and crime are kept fresh and up to date. Details of how this can be achieved are given in Chapter 9.

THE LONGER TERM CONSEQUENCES

The need for action to tackle all forms of violent or aggressive behaviour is widely recognized by staff who work in high-risk settings. Both they and their families live with the effects of incidents on an increasingly regular basis. Indeed, in every organization where I have been given an opportunity to work, staff who are at risk acknowledge that from their point of view the need is obvious.

Thankfully, an increasing number of companies are also beginning to recognize the benefits of taking action. In the longer term they have found that the payback includes:

- A better trained and more highly skilled workforce. Staff will be able to cope more easily with incidents while they are taking place, and respond more positively afterwards. As a result their stress levels will be lower and morale higher.
- Enhanced team spirit. A side effect of group de-briefing is that it significantly develops group cohesion. Somehow groups who have experienced adversity and satisfactorily negotiated any after-effects become much closer and stronger as a consequence.
- With aggression and abuse, improved customer relations. In many organizations 'care for the customer' initiatives are seen to be increasingly important. Staff who are able to defuse potentially aggressive customer contacts (before they get out of hand) will be able to offer a much better level of service than those who are not.

Although a cynic might argue that none of these benefits are measurable in terms of the 'bottom line', they are nevertheless highly significant, leading to improved staff performance both during and following incidents. However, perhaps the most convincing argument in favour of taking action can be found in the companies which carry out policies and practices to help staff who are at risk. Therefore the final three chapters which follow will be devoted to practical case studies of different organizational approaches. It will emerge that not only are the methods and staff involved different in each case but they also illustrate very different organizational settings.

SUMMARY

- There is no single ideal solution for how an organization should approach tackling aggression and abuse and violence and crime at work.
- Any approach that is adopted needs to be carefully thought through and planned.
- A comprehensive strategy for action will usually involve a number of preliminary actions, these include:
  - identifying an individual or group to take responsibility for the initiative
  - identifying the scope and seriousness of the problem
  - setting up a regular monitoring procedure
  - reviewing the information gathered and deciding where to start
- Options to tackle aggression and abuse could include:
  - reviewing the information available on common situations where incidents occur
  - taking preventative action to ensure incidents are kept to a minimum
  - designing and implementing staff training
  - monitoring the results
  - designing and implementing appropriate follow-up training
- Options to tackle violence and crime could involve:
  - reviewing security procedures and implementing any action to help minimize incidents
  - establishing an appropriate incident procedure
  - establishing a post-incident emergency response
  - establishing a longer term support framework
  - designing and implementing general staff training on coping and support skills

  – monitoring the results
  – designing and implementing appropriate ongoing training
- Although the organizational benefits of helping staff are difficult to measure in 'bottom-line' terms, they will lead to improved staff performance both during incidents and in the days and weeks that follow.

11

Organizational Case Study 1: The Leeds Permanent Building Society

INTRODUCTION

At the time of writing, the Leeds is the fifth largest building society in Britain with over 400 branches nationwide employing some 3500 field staff. Due to intense advertising and considerable work promoting its image, the Leeds is now a well-known household name.

It is also probably fair to say that in connection with robbery, the Leeds now has one of the most sophisticated and thorough training and support structures for staff. Indeed, in many respects it can be viewed as a model, highlighting in practice many of the points discussed in earlier chapters. Although the main focus for the service concerns raids on branches (usually armed raids), as we will see, the benefits have been shown to generalize and are also useful for staff who have to deal with abuse and aggression.

WHY WAS THE SERVICE STARTED?

As with many decisions in large organizations, the reasons

underlying why the Leeds chose to start some form of service for staff was influenced by a number of factors:

- Firstly, the Leeds has a long tradition of 'caring for staff'. This extends from the executive down through all levels of management.
- Secondly, following a major reorganization towards the end of the 1980s, senior area management were, on an increasingly regular basis, seeing the aftermath of incidents and the effects they had on branch staff.
- Also, since the mid-1980s building societies generally have experienced a progressive increase in the number of incidents taking place. The Leeds is no exception, and has received its fair share.
- Finally, throughout the 1980s there was a general rising tide of awareness of the need for counselling and support following involvement in a traumatic situation (in part influenced by the spate of major disasters which occurred during that time). Furthermore, within organizations there was a growing recognition of the role of Employee Assistance Programmes (EAPs) which had started to be imported from the States.

All of these factors combined to produce a very genuine concern at senior levels to do something to help branch staff who were in the front line. In 1989 this crystallized with the appointment of a Counselling Coordinator.

During the first year after appointment, the Counselling Coordinator carried out a comprehensive large-scale survey of branch staff. This probed practically every aspect of raids and their subsequent effects on employees, providing the foundation for David Richards (the current Counselling Coordinator) to develop the comprehensive procedure outlined below. There is no doubt that this stands as a tribute to David's efforts.

WHAT DOES THE LEEDS PROCEDURE INVOLVE?

Perhaps the easiest way of describing the Leeds support procedure is to follow the sequence of events once an incident has occurred (based on Richards[19]).

Stage 1. Immediate post-raid actions
Within seconds of an incident taking place the internal security department is automatically alerted through a very sophisticated alarm system. They in turn immediately call in the police. A side effect of this system is that all incidents are automatically monitored. Meanwhile, at the branch one member of staff will take responsibility for opening a sealed 'post-raid pack'. This contains:

- A procedural checklist of all of the actions that need to be carried out
- Contact cards giving the names and telephone numbers of both the local peer supporter and the Counselling Coordinator
- Supplies of a leaflet 'Coping with Robberies' which gives information about the likely reactions which victims may experience with what to do over the next few days

One of these packs is held in every branch in a prominent position where it can be easily accessed if needed.

Stage 2. Management support
Generally within the next hour (or two depending on the physical location of the branch) there will be a visit by a Senior Area Manager. Their role at this stage is to provide support in the immediate aftermath of the raid. As well as helping 'defuse' immediate staff reactions they will often help in more practical ways, e.g. driving staff home once police interviews are concluded—even simply making a cup of tea. (Note that the Counselling Coordinator is convinced that this stage is particularly important. It serves to underline, in a very real way, management concern.)

Stage 3. Peer support

The next stage (usually around the second or third day) involves one of a peer support group. These are ordinary branch staff who have received special training in the skills required to support victims. Each member of the support team looks after between 10 and 12 branches. They can be contacted by members of staff and will generally arrange to see victims outside normal working hours (usually at the victim's home).

Their work with victims is professionally supervised by one of the full-time counsellors (there are now two) and the content of any discussion is strictly confidential. No information is passed back to management without the explicit permission of the victim.

If appropriate, around this time victims will be gently encouraged to start a graded re-entry back to normal duties, though not necessarily immediately back to the duty they carried out at the time of the raid.

Stage 4. Incident de-briefing

Within two to three days of the incident, the staff involved are brought together (during normal work hours) for group de-briefing. At the Leeds this is now normal organizational routine following a raid. The de-briefing itself follows the critical incident pattern and is always carried out by one of the professional counsellors. Where, for one reason or another, it proves impossible to arrange group de-briefing within a reasonable time-scale, everyone who was involved is contacted by a counsellor and individually assessed for whether they need further help.

Stage 5. Psychological health screening

The start of de-briefing also marks the start of psychological health screening. Prior to any group discussion, at the start of de-briefing the staff complete a set of psychological health questionnaires.†

---

† The psychological health questionnaires which the Leeds counsellors use for screening staff include:
- The Impact of Events Scale[20]
- The General Health Questionnaire[21]

The results are used by the counsellors to assess whether individual members of staff are more seriously affected and will need further support. The questionnaires are also repeated at various points:

- The next day (to monitor the immediate effect of de-briefing)
- 1 week later
- 1 month later
- 3 months later
- 6 months later
- 1 year later
- 2 years later

The results of this pattern of longer term screening allow the counsellors to monitor the progress of victims and at the same time allow them to pick up any longer term problems. In instances where a branch is subject to a subsequent incident while screening is taking place, the whole procedure starts again from the beginning.

Stage 6. Longer term peer support
Following de-briefing and initial assessment, if necessary, victims may be referred to a member of the peer support group for ongoing help. Again, all contact with the supporter is closely supervised by one of the counsellors and (as would be expected) is entirely confidential.

Stage 7. Positive management gestures
At some point after the first few days, senior local management write to everyone involved and arrange for some other gesture to take place, e.g. arranging an evening meal at a local restaurant.

Stage 8. More intensive counselling/therapy for anyone seriously affected
Individuals who are seriously affected are identified either through contact with the peer supporter or through the psychological

screening process. Where this is the case, the individual is offered more intensive professional counselling/therapy.† Frequently this will also involve liaison with the individual's GP.

A schematic overview of the Leeds procedure is given in Fig. 11.1. However, it is important to emphasize that the procedure is automatic for all staff who are involved in an incident. Furthermore, if needed, support is also extended to the immediate families of victims. Indeed, the Leeds has even produced a leaflet for friends and families of staff which highlights what they can do to help in the event of an incident.

At present, the two counsellors confine their activities primarily to work concerned with dealing with incidents in branches. The wider question of whether the Leeds will open up the service to provide more general workplace counselling has yet to be addressed. For the present the counsellors take the view that it is more important to make sure their approach to dealing with robbery is fully effective before considering the implications of any expansion to the service.

As stated at the outset, the Leeds support procedure is commendably thorough. Indeed, it is highly unlikely that anyone would slip through the net. However, this is not the end of the story; in order for the procedure to work effectively there has also been considerable investment in training. This will be the topic that we will address next.

TRAINING AT THE LEEDS

Training at the Leeds takes place at a number of levels. It includes:

- Training for branch staff to prepare them for the possibility of a raid—in a sense 'stress inoculation' training

---

† The particular approach used by the Leeds counsellors for providing more intensive help is based on cognitive behavioural therapy (CBT). The counsellors point out that current research indicates that this approach outperforms any other therapy available (including drug treatment).

INCIDENT
↓
Post-raid pack
Procedural checklist
support contact numbers
'Coping with robberies' leaflet
↓
Local management visit
'Defusing'
practical help as needed
↓
Peer support
Peer supporters available,
gradual re-entry to normal duty starts
↓
Incident de-briefing
Professionally facilitated,
usually involving a post-raid meeting with
initial individual assessments
↓
Psychological health screening
Using regular, standard measures
over an extended period of time
↓
Peer support
Professionally supervised,
available to families/partners if needed
↓
Positive management gestures
Letter and evening meal (involving partners)
↓
More intensive help if needed

Figure 11.1   The Leeds support procedure (adapted from Richards[19])

- Training for the senior area managers who visit branches within the first couple of hours of an incident taking place
- Extensive initial and ongoing training for the peer support group

Each of these areas of training merits further examination.

Training for branch staff

In any building society or bank staff at branch level are invariably in the front line of any incident. In response to this the counsellors at the Leeds have developed a highly innovative training package. The main aim of the package is to raise staff awareness about the possibility of being involved in an incident together with helping them develop more effective strategies for coping. It is designed to be delivered in the branch by the branch manager as part of normal training (i.e. a half hour every Wednesday morning). The formal training input takes up one training session in each month over four months, though this is supplemented by individual exercises which are carried out in the intervening periods.

The centre-piece of the package is a professionally produced video coupled with individual workbooks for staff. The video itself is in four parts to complement the four training sessions. They deal with:

- A low-key raid and sensible security measures
- A violent and noisy raid together with coping techniques
- The group de-briefing process
- Being involved in police and judicial processes

The individual workbooks provide staff with an array of practical exercises concerning security procedures and actions they may need to take in the event of a raid, e.g.:

- Exercises to become familiar with branch security equipment.
- Practising taking note of, and recording physical descriptions of people who come into the branch.
- Developing 'coping lines', i.e. a set of rehearsed mental

statements which members of staff can activate during a raid.
These will help them cope both successfully and safely.
- Thinking through the stages in managing a gradual re-entry to work following an incident.
- An exercise structured round a leaflet for friends and families of employees which encourages them to discuss at home how friends and family can help in the event of an incident.
- etc.

Perhaps, though, the most important thrust of the training is provided by the exercises to help staff develop constructive thought patterns in the event of a raid, i.e. 'coping lines'—messages that we tell ourselves when confronted by a threatening situation. Although at first sight this might seem to be a trivial way of helping, it does have a track record of success. People who have thought through what they would think and say if an incident occurred typically cope better in an actual incident than those who have not. It is the psychological equivalent to a preventative stress/trauma inoculation.

An interesting side effect of the training is that the 'coping lines' technique has also proved useful in other situations, e.g. coping with aggression and abuse. Staff have found that visualizing and thinking through their own 'coping lines' for aggressive and abusive situations works just as well as in a raid. Although not initially a direct intention, the spin-off effect is that staff are now also far more effective at dealing with more common incidents.

Training for area managers
In order to help area managers (or anyone else) who visit a branch in the immediate aftermath of a raid, the Leeds offers a specific short training programme. This takes up half a day and covers:

- An introduction to understanding anxiety
- Specific 'defusing' skills to help staff deal with shock
- More general strategies for helping staff who were involved

The central message put across during the programme is based on an acrostic:

L   *Listen*—to the staff without minimizing/discounting their experience.
E   *Empathize*—show that you understand.
E   *Educate*—if needed, provide direct guidance and advice.
D   *Do*—offer practical help.
S   *Support*—any emotional distress.

Even though brief, area managers have found the programme immensely useful. Prior to receiving any training they often felt uncomfortable and awkward when visiting a branch. Furthermore, they had no way of knowing whether what they said and did was helpful to staff or not. The programme not only equipped them with a few basic skills but also helped to allay their anxiety and boosted their confidence.

Training for the peer support group
Training for the peer support group has been more extensive and more intensive than with any other group. So far it has included:

- A one week introductory residential training programme which now includes sessions on:
  - the nature of anxiety and the effects of trauma
  - skills for interviewing victims, basic concepts, gathering information, problem solving and putting it all together
  - skills in handling emotions
  - the role of de-briefing
  - skills in anxiety management
  - intensive role-play exercises followed by individual feedback (around a half of the programme is devoted to these activities).

  Furthermore, as all of the peer support group are volunteers, time is set aside for individual interviews with the facilitators to talk through how the volunteers feel about being involved with this kind of work. This is carried out in such a way that volunteers can opt not to continue if they wish without fear of recrimination from the organization. Indeed, in the early programmes one or two did opt out at this stage; however, they remain firmly committed to the concept of peer support.

- A follow-up two and a half day residential training programme which deals with:
  - further skills in managing anxiety
  - how to conduct a behavioural assessment of an employee following an incident
  - equipping peer supporters to deliver basic information to help victims cope with insomnia, deal with nightmares and make a progressive graded re-entry back to work
  - knowledge and skills to recognize severe disturbances to mental health.
- Individual days for ongoing supervision and training every two to three months. These deal with ongoing issues and difficulties as they arise as well as providing a forum for further training and development.

COSTS AND BENEFITS OF THE SERVICE

From the previous description it is clear that the Leeds has invested heavily in setting up the support procedure. The costs include:

- Salaries, overhead expenses and administrative back-up for the two professional counsellors
- Training costs for all of the peer support group together with a small bursary in recognition of their work
- Capital costs to produce the training package for branch staff
- Costs of bringing in relief staff to run a branch in order that de-briefing can take place

All of this expenditure is directly measurable. However, the benefits, although considerable, are less easily measured. Nevertheless, they include:

- *Increased morale*   Robbery can have a devastating effect on morale (particularly in branches that are subject to multiple incidents). At the Leeds it is obvious that management are concerned. Furthermore, their concern amounts to more than just paying lip service; ongoing investment in the support activities actively demonstrates their concern. Following an incident staff are no longer alone; they now have access to professional help.
- *Re-building of branch teams*   Just as robbery can devastate morale, it can also fracture work teams. Victims who do not receive support commonly feel isolated, alone and 'different' to everyone else at work. By contrast, a by-product of group de-briefing is that work teams actually become more closely bonded and stronger teams as a result.
- *A more confident, more highly skilled workforce*   As a result of the training, branch staff are now more confident in their ability to cope with robberies. Also as a result of the transference of the training into other situations, they are also more skilled at dealing with more commonplace incidents such as aggression and abuse.
- *A healthier workforce*   Following from the increase in morale and confidence, staff are psychologically more healthy following incidents. As we have seen, when an incident does take place their mental health is monitored on a regular basis for an extended period. If problems do arise then professional help is at hand to deliver appropriate psychological guidance and support.

On balance, although the investment of resources is considerable, the benefits for the organization are felt to be even greater. Despite the massive changes that the organization has experienced during the late 1980s and 1990s, the Leeds continues in its tradition of 'caring for staff'.

AUTHOR'S COMMENTARY

There is no doubt that the procedure adopted at the Leeds illustrates a highly sophisticated and professional approach. In many respects it is quite exceptional. However, it is also clear that the level of investment needed to create such a system can only be undertaken by larger companies. It does require very significant expenditure which medium and smaller sized companies cannot afford. The danger in this is that companies who cannot contemplate such a level of investment may instead wash their hands of the whole subject and do nothing.

I can only stress that in my view this would be a mistake. The Leeds support procedure is superb, but there are other approaches as well (which the next two chapters will illustrate). Although not as thorough as at the Leeds, they still provide victims with much needed help.

12

Organizational Case Study 2: Argos plc

INTRODUCTION

As an organization, Argos is another household name. The 'Argos catalogue' is familiar to young and old and can be found in the majority of households throughout the United Kingdom. Over the last 20 years Argos has grown to become the largest retailer across many product lines while at the same time becoming the second largest jeweller in Britain. In terms of organizational growth its record is enviable. Currently Argos has 320 plus branches employing some 8500 retail staff (rising to around 20 000 over the Christmas period). There is no doubt that Argos has gained a reputation and profile that many would wish to emulate.

As one would expect, internally the Argos operation is lean and highly professional, yet in culture, procedure and practice there is an undercurrent of 'concern for staff'. However, like many high street retail operations, over the last few years Argos' staff have become the victims of violence and crime at a number of levels, ranging from terrorist bombs to abuse and aggression. In response the company has developed a cost-effective 'bottom-up' response procedure which draws in both resources and expertise as needed.

HOW WAS THE SERVICE STARTED?

Although a nationwide operation, Argos is still the kind of

organization where one or two individuals can make a real impact and initiate organizational change. Effectively this is what happened with respect to violence and crime. At the end of the 1980s the Company Security Manager (Ian Harley) became increasingly concerned about the level and effects of incidents across the company. Together with the Retail Personnel and Training Manager (Graham Ledward) they designed a questionnaire to find out the extent of the problem and obtained top-level approval for a survey to be carried out.

The questionnaire probed the extent and effects of incidents involving aggression, abuse and violence. Furthermore, it also sought to elicit information on both the facts of incidents (what actually happened) and how they were perceived by staff. As one would expect, this highlighted the wide range of different perceptions of similar types of incidents. For example, behaviour which may be considered not particularly abusive in areas where levels of aggression and violence are high is often perceived as very disturbing in areas where aggression and violence are more the exception. Similarly, the very rare event of being spat on was perceived as far more abusive by some people than being physically jostled about.

Before actually carrying out the survey, a brief article was placed in the staff newsletter which is distributed to all staff. This gently highlighted the company's concern about the effect of incidents, pointing out that a survey would be taking place and emphasizing that it would be a joint personnel/security initiative. Furthermore, particular care was taken over the style of the article to ensure it did not unnecessarily raise anxiety levels among staff. With this as a backcloth, in 1990 the survey took place and every retail outlet received staff questionnaires.

The results confirmed that the scale and extent of the problem was significantly greater than had been anticipated. In Graham Ledward's words, 'You don't know what's happening until you've carried out a survey. I recommend every company to do one.'

The results also presented Argos with the difficulty of classifying incidents so that the scale of response would be appropriate to the scale of any incident. However, thinking on this issue was heavily influenced by two particularly nasty terrorist bomb incidents. Despite the crude classification, Argos decided to distinguish between major incidents (such as terrorist attack and incidents involving violence) and more frequent incidents (such as abuse and loss of goods or money). However, it is important to stress that, in making this distinction, there is no suggestion that more frequent incidents do not affect staff. It is recognized that even relatively low-key events can affect some people quite badly. However, perhaps the easiest way of illustrating how this operates in practice is to look in more detail at the chain of events following an incident.

WHAT DOES THE ARGOS PROCEDURE INVOLVE?

As with the Leeds procedure, Argos has defined a sequence of stages to be followed depending on the size, scale and effects of an incident. These are illustrated diagrammatically in Fig. 12.1 and discussed in detail below.

Stage 1. Immediate post-incident response
Once an incident has occurred the local manager must decide whether it can be dealt with at local level or whether it is sufficiently serious to call in other help. Although in some respects this might be seen as an arbitrary decision, guidance is at hand in the form of a procedure manual which is held by all store managers. This gives full details on what to do in the event of:

- Robbery or other crime involving loss of goods or money
- Incidents involving serious violence or trauma
- Exceptional events (such as bomb incidents)

In any of these instances the procedure escalates immediately to the next level and others are called in to help. However, by far the most common incidents involve aggression and abuse. These are normally dealt with at local level by the manager. Having said this

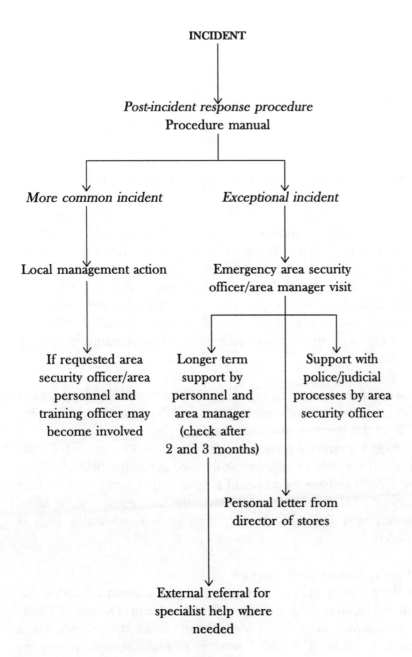

Figure 12.1   The Argos support procedure

it is important to emphasize that the manager is not alone in this work. Should the need arise he or she can request help from other more highly trained staff (e.g. security and personnel staff) where for some reason an individual is particularly affected by an incident. This type of support will continue for as long as needed.

In the event of a more serious incident, other stages in the response procedure swing into effect.

Stage 2. Emergency visit by the Area Security Officer and Area Manager
With more serious incidents, the first people to arrive at the scene from the field operation will be the Area Security Officer and the Area Manager. Typically they will arrive within the first few hours following the incident (and always within 24 hours for even the most distant locations). Their role is threefold: firstly, they provide immediate help and support for any staff who were involved; secondly, they will establish the scale of any loss; and, thirdly, they will help to get the business back into normal operation as quickly as possible.

Stage 3. Involvement by the Area Personnel and Training Officer
Generally within 48 hours the Area Personnel and Training Officer will become involved. This completes what Argos refer to as their tripartite approach to staff support. The area staff have received training in support skills and, generally, between them are able to address the needs of around 95 per cent of staff victims without recourse elsewhere. Usually the help given is short term, though in a few cases longer term or more specialist help is needed.

Stage 4. Longer term support
In the minority of cases where longer term support is needed this will be facilitated by the Area Personnel and Training Officer. Furthermore, even when victims appear to recover quickly a check is made at 2 and 3 months to make sure there are no delayed effects. Also, with particularly nasty incidents, special

support arrangements are made available around the first anniversary of the incident.

In cases where members of staff are required to assist with police enquiries or give evidence in court, an Area Security Officer will be available to help. Many of the security staff are themselves ex-police officers and are fully conversant with both police and court procedures. This puts them in an ideal position to provide guidance for staff who have to attend an identity parade or go into the witness box.

Finally, it is also worth mentioning that a few days after any incident all staff who were involved receive a personal letter from the Director of Stores emphasizing the Argos commitment to helping them recover as quickly as possible.

Stage 5. More professional help
Although the tripartite area team is able to support and help the vast majority of staff victims, from time to time (usually with more serious cases) more specialist help is needed. This is made available through referral to outside agencies such as Victim Support as and when needed.

By way of general comments it is worth noting that the Argos support procedure is available for any staff who are affected by an incident—both victims and witnesses. Furthermore, should the need arise, this is expanded to include temporary staff (over peak periods like Christmas) and any immediate family of members of staff. However, in kind with the Leeds, the service is not designed to help any members of the general public who may become involved. This exclusion is not through lack of concern but more a desire to avoid the potential complications that could arise from such action.

TRAINING IN ARGOS

Training is an important feature of the Argos approach. Effectively the types of training offered can be split into three separate initiatives:

- Training for store managers
- Training for the area support team
- Staff training

Each of these categories will be considered in turn.

Training for store managers

From the previous discussion it is clear that local store managers play a central role in helping staff to deal with the effects of more frequent incidents like aggression, abuse and (sometimes) overt violence. Their development and training for this role has been at three levels:

- Basic support skills training as part of normal management training
- Formal briefing on the operation and practice of the incident procedure, coupled with group discussions to clarify and resolve any particular difficulties
- Ongoing individual dialogue, support and guidance from the Area Personnel and Training Officer

Other than the briefing on the incident procedure, staff support in Argos is promoted as part of every manager's role. Training and ongoing help with the skills involved is part of the normal management development (rather than an exceptional activity). In turn this type of approach has helped to build a supportive culture where the majority of frequent incidents are contained and dealt with at store level.

Training for the Area Support Team

The Area Support Team generally only become involved with cases following particularly serious incidents or at the request of a store manager. As one would expect, their training has been considerably more extensive than that for store managers. To date, two complementary types of training have been carried out:

- An initial three day training programme delivered by external consultants, focusing on building a foundation of basic skills and knowledge, e.g.:
  - identifying the need for counselling and support
  - a model of the counselling process
  - basic counselling and support skills (including opportunities for practice)
  - guidance on when to seek external help
- A second one day training event delivered by the Victim Support Crime at Work Training Group. Whereas the first event focused primarily on basic skills this second event concentrated on:
  - the impact and effects of violence and crime
  - a model of crisis and change
  - the role of the Area Support Team
  - skills needed—knowledge and practice
  - prolonged or worrying reactions
  - other sources of support
  - specific company issues

Staff training
This is the next area of training which Argos intend to tackle in the near future. Currently a project team is working on a video-based training package to be delivered in-store by the manager dealing with 'ways of defusing aggression and violence'.

COSTS AND BENEFITS OF THE SERVICE

Although the costs involved in setting up and running the Argos procedure are not as extensive as at the Leeds, there has still been a very significant investment of both time and resources. This has included:

- All of the costs involved in designing, distributing and analysing the survey questionnaires
- Training/briefing costs for managers, staff and the Area Support Team
- Costs involved in designing the response procedure and subsequently producing the procedure manuals
- Costs involved in carrying out the response procedure (principally the time needed from the Support Team)

However, by contrast, the benefits far outweigh the costs, e.g.:

- Increased morale and sense of teamwork at store level
- Reinforcement of the store manager's position, not only in day-to-day management of staff but also as the first 'port of call' for help in the event of an incident
- Increased confidence for area staff when following up incidents

Furthermore, although there is no way of proving this point, had the support procedure not been in place Graham Ledward is convinced that, following two major bomb incidents, Argos would still be suffering the costs of extended sickness-absence from some staff.

AUTHOR'S COMMENTARY

As stated at the outset, the Argos procedure illustrates a cost-effective bottom-up approach to providing support. Each local manager deals with everyday incidents as far as they are able, calling on area help as needed. Similarly, the area team deal with more serious incidents as far as they are able, calling on external help as needed. However, the need for external help is usually minimal. Through careful forethought, planning and training, the Argos approach demonstrates how much can be achieved by existing staff. Specialist help is available if needed, but by far the majority of incidents are dealt with in-house. Although, as we have seen, there has been some investment of resources to set up the procedure, Argos offers a support model that works well within a large company but could also prove to be well within the reach of medium and smaller sized companies.

13

Organizational Case Study 3: A County Council Residential Children's Centre

INTRODUCTION

The third case illustration provides several interesting contrasts to the earlier examples:

- Firstly, it is drawn from the public rather than the private sector.
- Secondly, it illustrates how much can be achieved in smaller organizational settings.
- Finally, the support procedure specifically attempts to address how to provide personal support for staff victims, even when they may have contravened security/safety procedures.

The focus for the case study is Redsands Children's Centre, which is owned and operated by Cheshire County Council. The staff at Redsands educate and take care of 30 young people (mainly between the ages of 14 and 17) on a residential basis. It is important to note that Redsands has to operate 24 hours a day, 7 days a week, 52 weeks a year. Furthermore, unlike many other organizational settings, when a particular number of staff are needed on duty, then that number must be on duty; any absences must be covered by someone else. Organizationally Redsands is structured around five house units (one of which is a secure unit), each housing six young people. As a result some 27 staff will be required to work at each point during the day.

Although dealing with violence is not necessarily part of the work of staff, it has to be recognized that there is always a potential for violence. Many of the young people who are in residence come from seriously disturbed backgrounds and as a result may become prone to violent outbursts. Furthermore, most reports and Government inquiries into residential child care tend to concentrate on the needs of residents, sometimes ignoring the needs of staff. As a consequence, when incidents do occur staff tend to feel blamed or 'at fault' for causing or contributing to an incident.

This case study seeks to redress the balance. Here the focus is more towards the needs of members of staff. Having said this it is also probably fair to say that Cheshire County Council and Redsands in particular provide an excellent example of how both the needs of staff and the needs of young residents can both be met. The approach discussed here addresses the needs of staff victims without abandoning an overall child-centred framework. However, as we will see, integrating the needs of staff as well does require careful forethought and planning.

WHY WAS THE SERVICE STARTED?

Towards the end of the 1980s senior management at Redsands started to investigate the causes of low morale among staff. At that time this manifested in general disillusionment, high levels of staff turnover (some choosing to leave the profession altogether), difficulty in attracting qualified staff to replace those who left and high levels of sickness absence. Indeed, it is perhaps worth pointing out that in small establishments any absence has an immediate and obvious effect on the workload of remaining members of the team. As a result group cohesion within the team was placed under immense strain, in turn creating a downward spiral on morale generally.

Roy Grimwood, the Principal of Redsands, together with his management team felt that something had to be done to identify and address the underlying causes of low morale (rather than merely addressing the obvious symptoms such as sickness absence rates). In order to do this, two workshops focusing on 'staff care' were arranged. These involved senior managers from the whole of South Cheshire Social Services District (of which Redsands is a part). However, the outcome of the first District workshop for Redsands was to identify six contributory causes of low morale which were in need of urgent attention. These were:

- The public image of the centre
- Violence towards staff
- Staff burnout
- The stress associated with disciplinary hearings
- Unclear and unrealistic expectations
- Frustration with training

Between the two workshops the Redsands management group undertook projects to start to tackle each of these issues. However, rather than describing each in detail, here we will concentrate solely on the work carried out in respect of violence towards staff.

As an aside which will have relevance later, another outcome from the first workshop (instigated by another group) was the formation of a team of volunteer counsellors who would be available to the Social Work Department as a whole. Furthermore, all of the members of this team were trained and experienced in counselling across a very wide range of issues.

In the meantime, the Redsands management group came to the conclusion that what was needed was a more proactive approach which acknowledged the threat of violence as an inherent feature of day-to-day working life. Furthermore, unlike other organizational settings (such as banks, building societies, shops, etc.) where most incidents are carried out by people who are external to the organization, incidents in a residential home are significantly different, e.g.:

- Firstly, principally they occur as a result of violent outbursts by young residents.
- Secondly, despite the type of incident that occurs, at some stage the relationship between the member of staff and his or her assailant will need to be rebuilt and contact re-established.
- Thirdly, in this type of setting any incident necessarily involves an in-depth inquiry to determine precisely what happened. Also, in instances where staff may have mismanaged a situation or been at fault in some way, it could lead to suspension and/or disciplinary action.

Clearly all of these factors had to be taken into account in creating an appropriate staff support procedure. What emerged as a result is described in the section that follows.

WHAT DOES THE REDSANDS PROCEDURE INVOLVE?

As with the previous case studies, perhaps the easiest way of illustrating the Redsands procedure is to follow the sequence of events once an incident has taken place (these are also shown diagrammatically in Fig. 13.1).

Stage 1. Immediate post-incident actions
(a) As staff are always on duty in a house unit in pairs (or trios), the other member of staff attends and helps to mediate/defuse the situation. If necessary he or she can call for further help from other staff on site at very short notice.
(b) The manager/senior member of staff on duty will, as soon as practicable, assess the situation and make decisions about any further action. In more serious incidents where a member of staff needs to be taken home or to hospital for medical

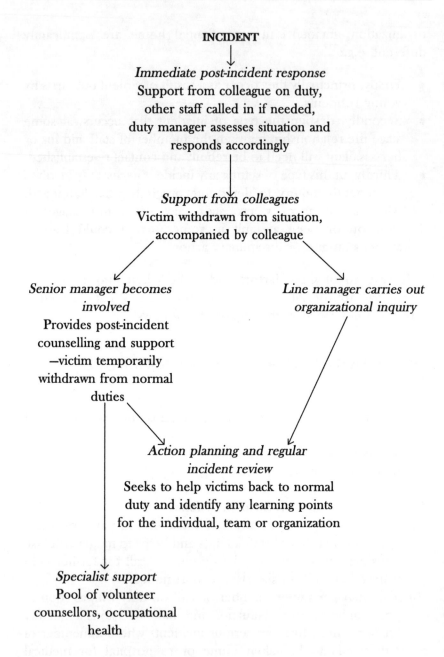

Figure 13.1   The Redsands support procedure

attention, the manager will also make sure that he or she is accompanied by a colleague.

Stage 2. Support from colleagues
In order to help defuse shock reactions to an incident, the staff victim is quickly withdrawn from the immediate environment where the incident took place and given time to recover. Throughout this period of withdrawal they are accompanied by a colleague whose primary role is to provide post-incident personal support. With more serious incidents staff victims are given the option of going home if they wish (however, it is interesting to note that only in the most serious cases is the option actually taken up). Beyond this point the procedure splits into two parallel courses of action (see Fig. 13.1 for further clarification).

Stage 3. Subsequent actions
The next stage in the Redsands procedure recognizes that, in this particular organizational setting, two separate sets of needs must be met. Firstly, there are the personal needs of staff victims for support and help to recover from the incident; secondly, there is a managerial and organizational need to find out precisely what happened so that appropriate action can be taken with either the resident, the member of staff, the staff team or the organization. Furthermore, the procedure acknowledges that each of these needs are best dealt with separately. Hence at this stage two managers become involved:

(a) The role of the first of the two managers is concerned exclusively with the needs of the staff victim. Post-incident counselling and support is offered in order to help them come to terms with their experience. Furthermore, when appropriate, the victim will also be helped to construct an action plan for returning to normal working. It is important to note that the manager who carries out this role is not the victim's own line manager. This ensures that the support manager has some degree of freedom to provide personal support without being concerned (or directly involved) with any investigatory aspect of the incident.

At Redsands this role is usually carried out by the Assistant Principal (Training and Development), Sue Clifton. As a matter of course Sue also ensures that staff victims are informed about other sources of help within the Authority, e.g. Occupational Health and the team of volunteer counsellors.

(b) Given that the personal needs of the victim are being adequately addressed, the victim's line manager is then free to investigate the incident as part of normal managerial procedure. The primary concern here is to establish what happened and how to get the staff victim and/or team back to normal working again. Also, as a matter of course, all incidents are fully documented for later review.

Stage 4. More specialist support

In a very small number of cases, where the effects of an incident prove more serious, the support manager (or victim themself) can call/request further help from two other sources available within the wider County Council structure. These are, firstly, the Occupational Health Department (for medical issues) and, secondly, the pool of volunteer counsellors mentioned earlier. This group have now produced a booklet giving the names of the counsellors, how they can be contacted and their respective area of expertise; this is available for both managers and staff. It is also important to point out that staff victims can approach either of these two groups immediately—with or without the knowledge of management.

Stage 5. Action planning

The final stage of the Redsands procedure involves identifying what can be learned as a result of any incident(s) and planning appropriate action for the future. All incident reports are reviewed on a regular basis by the management team and, as appropriate, a wide variety of different types of action are taken, e.g.:

- Providing additional support for either individual members of staff or residents
- Further training and development for staff
- Withdrawing a team from very high-risk situations for a brief period of respite—particularly after nasty incidents or lengthy stressful periods
- Where other staff are used to cover any absence following an incident, ensuring there is an adequate period of overlap when the permanent member of staff returns to work so that they can readjust gradually to their normal work role.

Although there would appear to be an inherent conflict between this policy and a results-oriented approach to management, in practice this does not prove to be the case. With sensible management, it is possible for concerns about 'staff care' and 'achieving results' to coexist without conflict.

Finally, it is important to highlight that the whole thrust of this procedure is to address the needs of *everyone* who was involved in an incident, ensuring that:

- Residents have a fair opportunity to present their side of the story.
- Staff victims are adequately supported rather than just blamed.
- The operation gets back to normal functioning as soon as possible.

TRAINING AND DEVELOPMENT AT REDSANDS

The focus of training and development at Redsands has been very different to the approach adopted by either Argos or the Leeds. Indeed, in many respects the skills needed for supporting and helping victims are part and parcel of the basic training for most social workers. What is different is who the skills are used to help.

At the time this initiative was started, listening, counselling and support skills were used primarily to help clients of the service (i.e. young residents). However, the prevailing organizational culture between team members (and managers) was more one of 'we don't get stressed—we survive'. This lack of acknowledgement of the pressure and stress involved in the work led to a highly charged, dysfunctional undercurrent which led to the symptoms (such as high absence rates) described earlier. What was needed was a broad organizational development approach rather than training courses on skills which were already well developed.

It is also worth noting that the situation at Redsands probably mirrors the classic dilemma in many care (and custodial) settings, i.e. 'Who helps the helpers when they are in need?' Although a gross generalization, it is probably fair to comment that organizations are often very good at meeting the needs of their primary customers/clients, but often have a 'blind spot' towards their own staff.

As was mentioned in the introduction, the start of the organizational development initiative was the two workshops for the management team. These provided a forum for the team to reflect on the current situation, identify the key areas that needed attention and start to plan appropriate action. However, in retrospect, Roy Grimwood identifies the crucial point as a shift in managerial thinking which allowed them to acknowledge and talk about the stress and pressure within the job—both their own and those of their staff (without being castigated as 'soft' or 'not coping'). This led directly to the six specific initiatives mentioned earlier. With respect to violence, once the procedure had been clarified and put into effect, it gave permission for both staff and management to:

- Be more open and honest about the impact of incidents
- Be more openly supportive and caring of one another

As we will see in the section that follows, the benefits that flowed from this were quite far reaching. However, as Roy Grimwood points out, 'It is necessary to put in effort to sustain the procedure, otherwise it tends to be forgotten.'

COSTS AND BENEFITS OF THE SERVICE

As the basic skills required for running a victim support service were already in place, the costs of setting up the Redsands support procedure were relatively small. They include:

- Costs associated with setting up and running the initial two workshops
- Costs associated with managerial and staff time for supporting victims of violence
- Occasional additional costs such as paying for someone to work alongside a staff victim in order to facilitate a graded re-entry to normal work after an incident and temporary costs for replacement staff while those working in high-risk situations take a period of respite

However, these have been greatly outweighed by the benefits, e.g.:

- More open communication. Even when they have been at fault, staff are now far more open and honest in disclosing their part in any incident.
- A significant reduction in the amount of time staff take to recover from incidents and, associated with this, a corresponding reduction in the time taken for them to return to normal duties.
- Following from the previous point, a significant reduction in levels of staff absence after an incident.
- Easier budgetary management. One direct consequence of staff taking less absence and returning to normal duties more quickly has been that the Centre can now operate comfortably within its budgetary targets; even though additional staff are used in a support capacity (e.g. during graded re-entry or during periods where staff exposed to high risk take a period of respite) the Centre does not lose out financially. This is partly because where staff do take extended sick leave then they have to be replaced; the nature of the work at Redsands is such that work cannot be allowed to pile up. If two staff are

needed for a particular duty then two staff have to be provided. Therefore, it follows that reducing sickness absence has very high implications for savings.

- General morale at the Centre has increased significantly; indeed, staff morale is now more affected by external pressures (which are outside their control) than by any internal events.

By virtue of the fact that resources did not have to be allocated to basic skills training, one could argue that the management and staff at Redsands started at a considerable advantage. Nevertheless, despite this the catalogue of benefits is still very impressive and a credit to their efforts.

AUTHOR'S COMMENTARY

In writing this section I am aware that the Redsands case study draws this text to a close. However, I am also aware that I could not ask for a better place at which to end. Redsands highlights so many points which for me have become so important, e.g.:

- Firstly, it illustrates that even in settings where basic support skills are an integral part of the job, unless the needs of staff are specifically addressed, they are likely to be overlooked.
- Secondly, it illustrates that even in settings where violence can be expected, it still has a debilitating (and costly) impact on victims.
- Thirdly, it demonstrates that even in cases where staff 'got it wrong' or did not follow safety procedures to the letter, care and support for their needs as victims need not be withheld. It is possible to design a support procedure that addresses both the needs of victims for support and the needs of the organization (even though this may result in disciplinary action).
- Fourthly, it highlights that providing support for victims can be equally effective in smaller organizational settings. It is not a

luxury that only large national and multi-national companies can enjoy.

- Finally, and perhaps most significant of all, Redsands highlights the cultural aspect of victim support. The crucial issue is one of organizational culture. Wherever organizations persist in maintaining 'macho' beliefs which ignore basic human needs then victims will continue to suffer unnecessarily. Acknowledging, accepting and supporting staff who are in need has to be a better alternative.

Appendix 1
Sources of further help

ORGANIZATIONS OFFERING SPECIFIC HELP WITH RESPONDING TO VIOLENCE AND CRIME AT WORK

Victim Support

Victim Support is the only national organization that offers a comprehensive service to victims of crime. Among their many activities they offer:

1. Support and information for victims of crime, carried out through a network of local groups covering most of England, Wales and Northern Ireland. Access to local services can be gained either via the National Office or through the police or by telephone—the local number will be listed in the telephone directory or can be obtained through directory enquiries or from the National Office.
2. A Witness Service in the Crown Courts to provide help for people who are required to give evidence in court.
3. Victim Support have also formed a 'Crime at Work Training Team' specifically to offer help to organizations who are addressing crime at work. This group can be contacted through the National Office:

Victim Support
National Office
Cranmer House
39 Brixton Road
London SW9 6DZ

Tel: 071 735 9166
Fax: 071 582 5712

Victim Support Scotland
14 Frederick Street
Edinburgh
EH2 2HB

Tel: 031 225 7779

Northern Ireland Federation of VSS
Room 308
Bryson House
28 Bedford St.
Belfast
N. Ireland BT2 7FE

Tel: 0232 244039

Westgate Specialist Training

The author's own training consultancy, with respect to violence
and crime at work, Westgate Specialist Training can provide:

1. Specialist consultancy help concerning:
   - monitoring and minimizing violence and crime
   - setting up internal company support networks for victims of
     violence and crime
2. Specific help with designing and producing training materials
   on minimizing and managing violence and crime or setting up
   an internal support network

3. Management/staff training and/or training in all of the areas of training discussed in Chapter 9

Westgate Specialist Training can be contacted through the author:

> Peter Reynolds
> Westgate Specialist Training
> 69 Westgate
> Tranmere Park
> Guiseley
> Leeds LS20 8HH
>
> Tel: 0943 873129

OTHER ORGANIZATIONS THAT MAY BE ABLE TO PROVIDE HELP AND ADVICE THOUGH NOT SPECIFICALLY WITH ISSUES CONCERNING VIOLENCE AND CRIME AT WORK

The Samaritans

Although the Samaritans are not specifically dedicated to supporting victims of violence and crime such cases do figure in their work. They are able to provide confidential support for anyone in need. This may be by telephone or face to face. Samaritans are a national organization with branches in most cities and large towns. Their local telephone number will be listed in the telephone directory or can be obtained through directory enquiries.

Citizens' Advice Bureaux

This is another national organization that may be useful for information and advice. A local telephone number will be listed in the telephone directory or can be obtained through directory enquiries.

The British Association for Counselling

BAC is one of the professional bodies for counsellors. They maintain a register of counsellors and can be contacted at:

> The British Association for Counselling
> 37a Sheep Street
> Rugby CV21 3BX

The British Psychological Society

The BPS is the professional body for psychologists. They have a specific division concerned with counselling psychology and also maintain a register of chartered psychologists. The BPS can be contacted at:

> The British Psychological Society
> 48 Princess Road East
> Leicester LE1 7DR
>
> Tel: 0533 549568
> Fax: 0533 470787

Appendix 2

Illustration training designs

EXAMPLE 1: A ONE DAY TRAINING PROGRAMME TO HELP STAFF MANAGE AGGRESSIVE AND ABUSIVE INCIDENTS MORE EFFECTIVELY

This example illustrates what can be achieved with a one day, off-the-job training programme. It was developed by the author and can be delivered either directly to 'front-line' employees or adapted as a trainer training event for staff who wish to present similar types of programmes.

Managing aggression and abuse

Designed for: Front-line staff who may have to deal with aggressive or abusive incidents during the course of their work

Duration: One day, off-the-job

Number of participants: 10 to 12

Training objectives: By the end of the programme participants should be able to:
— identify and appreciate the different types of situations or circumstances that can lead to

frustration and anger.
— take action (as far as they are able) to change any physical causes of frustration
— identify the early warning signs that some one is becoming potentially aggressive.
— adapt their behaviour to 'defuse' frustrating or aggressive incidents before they erupt into overt violence.

Programme pre-work:

Prior to attending this programme participants should think about, and make a few notes on:
— the types of incidents that take place where they work
— how they currently manage such incidents
— what aspects of managing aggression and abuse they find difficult

Outline schedule of events

0900–0930	Introductions
	Programme objectives
	Overview of the activities involved

Causes of aggression at work

0930–0950	Small group exercise based on the following discussion question: 'What situations or circumstances lead to frustration, anger or abuse in your workplace?'
0950–1015	Feedback and discussion in large group coupled with input from the trainer on 'causes of frustration and aggression' (as needed)
1015–1030	Action planning—large group 'brainstorming' exercise based on: 'What action can we take to minimize or eradicate situations or circumstances that cause aggression at work?'
1030–1045	Morning coffee

Signs and symptoms of aggression

1045–1105	Small group exercise based on the following discussion question: 'What are the early indicators that someone is becoming increasingly frustrated or aggressive?'
1105–1130	Feedback and discussion in large group coupled with input from the trainer on 'warning signs of frustration and aggression' (as needed)

Techniques for defusing aggression

1130–1200	Small group exercise based on the following discussion question: 'Drawing from your pre-work, what strategies and techniques do you currently use to defuse people who are becoming frustrated and angry?'
1230–1330	Lunch
1330–1345	Recap and summary of defusing techniques

Defusing techniques in practice

1345–1600	Sequence of role-play exercises in trios to practise using defusing techniques in a variety of aggressive and abusive situations, followed by individual feedback (optional use of video). Afternoon tea to be taken at an appropriate point.

Dealing with difficulties

1600–1610	Exercise in pairs to review and reconsider the difficulties that participants identified in their pre-work
1610–1640	Large group discussion to clarify and resolve any outstanding difficulties
1640–1700	Open forum
	Programme review
	Close

EXAMPLE 2: A SERIES OF FOUR HALF-HOUR SESSIONS COUPLED WITH ADDITIONAL EXERCISES TO HELP STAFF MANAGE AGGRESSION AND ABUSE

Like the previous illustration, this example tackles the same subject. However, in this case it is specifically aimed at organizations that choose to incorporate this type of training within their normal ongoing training framework—in particular shops and offices that set aside half an hour every week for staff training.

The design is intended to be delivered by the manager (or whoever is responsible for staff training) in any work setting. Therefore it will require detailed support materials for the trainer inputs, discussion topics and interim activities. Furthermore, given the time restrictions, it cannot treat the topic as thoroughly as in Example 1. Nevertheless, it will still provide a useful platform for staff to develop their skills.

Finally, as with Example 1, the programme was developed by the author to be adapted to individual organizational circumstances. Furthermore, it can be modified to become a trainer training event for managers, supervisors or staff trainers who wish to deliver similar types of sessions.

Managing aggression and abuse

Designed for: Front-line staff who may have to deal with aggressive or abusive incidents during the course of their work

Duration: Four half-hour sessions, ideally carried out at the rate of one every two or three weeks

Number of participants: Normal work groups

Training objectives: By the end of the programme participants should be able to:

– identify aspects of their workplace that trigger (or exacerbate) frustration and anger.
– take action (as far as they are able) to change any physical causes of frustration.
– identify the early warning signs that someone is becoming potentially aggressive.
– adapt their behaviour to 'defuse' frustrating or aggressive incidents before they erupt into overt violence.

Programme pre-work:

During the two to three weeks prior to undertaking the four training sessions, staff should keep a record of all of the instances that lead to aggression and abuse (or alternatively where aggression is common, the record should include a representative sample of instances). In particular, they should keep a note of:

– what triggered the incident.
– any aspects of the incident they found difficult to deal with.

Outline schedule of events

Session 1
- Overview of the four sessions.
- Discussion based on the pre-work reviewing the types of incidents that have taken place, in particular highlighting any physical aspects of the workplace that trigger (or exacerbate) frustration and aggression.
- Brief 'brainstorming' exercise to generate ideas for modifying the workplace to reduce frustration and aggression, followed by highlighting those ideas that can be put into effect immediately and those that would need more senior approval.
- Introduce interim activity 1.

Interim activity 1
- Carry out any minor changes in the workplace as agreed in session 1 and/or submit a request or proposal for more extensive change (for changes that require external approval).
- Individual exercise for staff designed to help them identify and record the early indicators of frustration and aggression.

Session 2
- Report back on progress with any workplace modifications.
- Drawing on staff responses to interim activity 1, discussion on the early indicators of frustration and aggression, with trainer input as required.
- Drawing on staff responses to the pre-work, discussion to highlight and record what aspects of incidents staff find difficult to manage.
- Introduce interim activity 2.

Interim activity 2
- Individual exercise for staff to help them monitor and record how they currently attempt to defuse potentially aggressive situations.

Session 3
- Brief report back on the results of interim activity 2.
- Introduction to defusing skills for minimizing frustration and aggression, in particular covering staying calm, appropriate body language and basic listening skills, e.g. reflecting, paraphrasing and summarizing.
- Practise in pairs so that staff can try out the basic defusing skills.
- Introduce interim activity 3.

Interim activity 3
- Exercise designed to help staff use basic defusing skills during the normal course of their work. The exercise will also prompt them to reflect on their experience in order to identify how effective it has been in practice.

Session 4
- Brief report back on the results of interim activity 3.
- Continuation of defusing skills, in particular covering the technique of negative enquiry.
- Practise in pairs so that staff can try out using negative enquiry.
- Discussion aimed at clarifying and if possible resolving any final issues.
- Introduce final activity to help staff use negative enquiry during the course of their work.

Note that, although not part of the managing aggression sessions, at some later stage it would be worth spending a few minutes checking out how staff feel once they have had a chance to use defusing skills in an actual incident.

EXAMPLE 3: A SERIES OF FOUR HALF-HOUR SESSIONS COUPLED WITH ADDITIONAL EXERCISES TO ENABLE STAFF TO RESPOND POSITIVELY BOTH DURING AND AFTER A VIOLENT INCIDENT

Like the previous illustration, this example is designed to be delivered by a manager or supervisor as part of ongoing staff training. It couples two of the areas discussed in Chapter 8, i.e. how to respond in the event of an incident and skills for helping afterwards.

Responding positively to violence at work

Designed for: Front-line staff who may become involved in violent incidents during the course of their work

Duration: Four half-hour sessions, ideally carried out at the rate of one every two or three weeks

Number of
participants: Normal work groups

Training
objectives:

By the end of the training staff should be able to:
— minimize any danger both to themselves and others
— implement their own personal coping strategy
— implement the company's incident and post-incident procedure(s)
— implement skills that aid recovery
— recognize when to seek further help

Programme
pre-work:

Prior to attending the training sessions staff should have read and become conversant with the company's incident and post-incident procedure(s)

Outline schedule of events

Session 1
- Overview of the four sessions.
- Brief introduction and review of the company's incident and post-incident procedure(s), followed by a practical exercise to simulate using the procedure(s) in the event of an incident.
- General discussion to clarify and resolve any confusions or difficulties.
- Introduce interim activity 1.

Interim activity 1
- Exercise designed to prompt staff to think about (and make notes on) what they think they could do to:
  — minimize any danger both to themselves and others in the event of an incident.
  — minimize the personal impact of an incident.

Session 2
- Discussion and review of staff responses to interim activity 1, focusing on:
    - minimizing danger to themselves and others.
    - ideas on what people can do to help themselves cope during an incident.
- Introduce concept of 'personal coping strategies'.
- Practical exercise to help staff develop their own personal coping strategy.
- Introduce interim activity 2.

Interim activity 2
- Practical exercise for staff to try out implementing their personal coping strategy with any hostile or aggressive situation which arises during the course of their work.

Session 3
- Discussion and review of staff reactions following implementation of their personal coping strategy.
- Further practice on coping strategies in action.
- Introduce other self-help and support skills.
- Introduce interim activity 3.

Interim activity 3
- Individual exercise for staff to think through and record the steps involved to facilitate a graded re-entry to normal work following a violent incident.

Session 4
- Discussion and review of staff responses to interim activity 3.
- Continuation of work on self-help and support skills.
- Brief exercise to highlight 'when and where to seek help', including trainer input as required.

EXAMPLE 4: A TWO AND A HALF HOUR TRAINING DESIGN FOR MANAGERS AND SUPERVISORS OF STAFF WHO MAY BECOME INVOLVED IN A VIOLENT INCIDENT

Example four seeks to equip line managers and supervisors with basic support skills to enable them to provide constructive help for staff who have been involved in a serious incident at work. The actual design is limited to two and a half hours to enable it to be added on to a normal management meeting.

Supporting staff victims

Designed for: Line managers and/or supervisors of staff who are at risk from violence and crime at work

Duration: Two and a half hours

Number of participants: 6 to 12

Training objectives: By the end of the training participants should be able to:
— identify and respond to the normal range of reactions which staff may experience following an incident where they work.
— provide basic day-to-day support for staff victims in order to help facilitate their return to normal working.
— recognize (and respond appropriately) when staff victims display obvious symptoms indicating they need to be referred for more specialist help.

Programme pre-work: Prior to attending this training session participants should have read a pre-prepared document outlining:

— typical reactions of victims following involvement in a violent incident and
— skills that help victims recover.

Outline schedule of events

Approximate timing	Activity
10 min	Introduction and overview of the training session
10 min	Small group exercise (drawing on pre-work) to clarify and summarize the range of individual effects in the days and weeks following involvement in a serious incident
15 min	Plenary discussion to review small group work (coupled with tutor input as appropriate)
10 min	Brief plenary discussion drawing on pre-work to introduce basic support skills
40 min	Various practical exercises to help participants develop and consolidate the support skills highlighted earlier
20 min	Small group exercise to identify when to consider referring a victim for more specialist help
30 min	Plenary discussion to review small group work (coupled with tutor input as appropriate)
15 min	Final questions, summary and close

EXAMPLE 5: A HALF-DAY TRAINING PROGRAMME FOR STAFF WHO BECOME INVOLVED WITH VICTIMS AND/OR WITNESSES DURING THE FIRST FEW HOURS AFTER A SERIOUS INCIDENT

Chapter 7 highlighted the fact that when confronted by a violent or traumatic situation, typically people go into a short-term automatic shock reaction. While in this condition they may act in uncharacteristic or unexpected ways. It follows therefore that, as a minimum, anyone who is involved with victims (or witnesses) during this time must be skilled in defusing shock. This is the central objective of the following short training event.

Effective emergency response skills

Designed for: Any member of staff who becomes involved with victims and/or witnesses during the first few hours after an incident

Duration: Half-a-day, off-the-job

Number of participants: 6 to 10

Training objectives: By the end of the training participants should be able to:

— recognize when people are exhibiting a shock reaction.
— take appropriate action to defuse shock.
— provide appropriate practical help as needed.
— recognize when to request more specialist help.

Programme pre-work: Prior to attending the training, participants should have read a pre-prepared document outlining:

— details of the shock reaction and likely behaviour that people may exhibit as a result, together with,
— behaviour that may require more specialist support.

Outline schedule of events

08.45–09.00   Introduction and overview of the course

What is shock?

09.00–09.20   Small group exercise drawing on the course
                    pre-work and participants' personal experience
                    to identify and record:
                    — What is shock?
                    — How people often behave when in shock.

09.20–09.40   Plenary discussion to review small group work
                    (coupled with tutor input as appropriate)

Skills for defusing shock

09.40–09.55   Small group exercise to identify skills that help
                    people deal with shock effectively

09.55–11.15   Skills practice—various exercises (coupled with
                    individual feedback) in pairs and trios to
                    develop, consolidate and extend participants'
                    skills in helping defuse people in shock

Providing practical help

11.15–11.35   Large group 'brainstorming' exercise to identify
                    what types of practical help staff in shock might
                    need

When to seek specialist help

11.35–11.50   Small group exercise drawing on both the
                    course pre-work and participants' personal
                    experience, to identify the circumstances
                    where more specialist help might be needed

11.50–12.10   Plenary review of small group work (coupled
                    with tutor input as appropriate)

12.10–12.30   Open forum, summary and close

EXAMPLE 6: A ONE DAY TRAINING DESIGN FOR STAFF WHO BECOME INVOLVED WITH VICTIMS ON A MORE FORMAL (OR LONGER TERM) BASIS

This training design is based on a one day programme developed by the Victim Support Crime at Work Group. One particularly innovative feature is the use of 'role groups' (i.e. groups comprised of participants from common occupational roles within an organization, such as security staff, personnel, etc.) to examine both the extent of their involvement with victims and any gaps in the support provision.

Crime at work

Designed for: Managers, specialist staff or others who become involved with victims of incidents on a more formal basis (e.g. as part of an 'in-house' victim support network)

Duration: One day, off-the-job

Number of participants: 6 to 12

Training objectives: By the end of the training participants should be able to:

— recognize the impact and effects of violence and crime on victims.

— apply appropriate models of crisis and change to help victims within their own work setting.

— identify how the different organizational roles can contribute to supporting victims.

— implement basic support skills with victims.

— identify both where and when to seek additional support (perhaps from outside of the organization).

Outline schedule of events

09.30–09.45	Introductions and expectations for the day
09.45–10.15	Pairs exercise and plenary review: — defining the scope of the problem — determining participants' level of experience — outlining and discussing 'official' definitions of violence and crime
10.15–11.30	Small group work and plenary review — examining the impact and effects of crime — developing and discussing an appropriate response model
11.30–12.30	Role groups and plenary review: — examining 'what is my/our role?' — developing and discussing an appropriate response model
12.30–13.15	Lunch
13.15–14.30	Role groups: — 'What other help/support is needed?'
14.30–17.15	Various group exercises and plenary review: — developing and extending skills — defining the range of additional support needed — outlining the help offered by Victim Support — identifying prolonged or worrying reactions — identifying any company issues for feedback
17.15–17.30	Open forum and final questions Review of course objectives Summary and close

EXAMPLE 7: A THREE DAY RESIDENTIAL TRAINING DESIGN FOR STAFF WHO BECOME INVOLVED WITH VICTIMS ON A MORE FORMAL (OR LONGER TERM) BASIS

This three day programme is based on a design developed by the author for a client organization in the financial services sector. By virtue that the programme is residential and longer than any of the earlier examples, more time is available for participants to develop practical skills for supporting victims.

Supporting victims of violence and crime

Designed for: Managers, specialist staff or others who become involved with victims of incidents on a more formal basis (e.g. as part of an 'in-house' victim support network)

Duration: Three days residential

Number of participants: 6 to 10

Training objectives: By the end of the training participants should be able to:
— offer a high level of support to victims and, when needed, their immediate families.
— respond constructively to feelings and emotions expressed by victims.
— recognize and facilitate 'normal' recovery patterns.
— recognize when to seek more specialist help.
— make constructive use of supervision and support arrangements.

Programme pre-work: Prior to attending this training, participants should have completed a pre-prepared pre-work booklet giving details on:

 — the effects of violence and crime on victims
and witnesses
 — effective methods of responding
 — skills required for follow-up, de-briefing and
support
 — when to seek more professional help
 — how to make use of supervision and support

Outline schedule of events

Day 1
09.00–09.30   Introductions and ice-breaking

Clarifying expectations
09.30–10.00   Introductory exercise to help participants
clarify their expectations about the programme

The effects of violence and crime on victims
10.00–10.30   Small group exercise based on the programme
pre-work to help participants clarify their
understanding of the effects of violence and
crime
10.30–10.45   Morning coffee
10.45–11.45   Plenary review of small group work (coupled
with tutor input as appropriate)

Basic support skills
11.45–12.45   Small group exercise to define and describe
basic support techniques, followed by plenary
review (coupled with tutor input as appropriate)
12.45–13.45   Lunch

Support skills practice
13.45–15.30   Various exercises in pairs and trios to try out

	and practise basic skills for supporting victims
15.30–15.45	Afternoon tea
15.45–18.00	Continuation of support skills practice
18.00–19.30	Individual interviews—private study or individual work on personal learning journals

Day 2
| 09.00–09.30 | Work in pairs to reflect on personal learning from the previous day |

The de-briefing process
| 09.30–10.00 | Tutor input outlining the stages in the de-briefing process |

De-briefing practice
| 10.00–12.45 | Role-play/simulation exercises (coupled with video feedback) for participants to practise carrying out the de-briefing process (morning coffee to be taken at an appropriate point) |
| 12.45–13.45 | Lunch |

Handling emotions
13.45–14.15	Small group exercise to identify constructive techniques for helping victims who have been emotionally upset by an incident
14.15–18.00	Continuation of support skills and de-briefing practice (afternoon tea to be taken at an appropriate point)
18.00–19.30	Individual interviews—private study or individual work on personal learning journals

Day 3
| 09.00–09.30 | Work in pairs to reflect on personal learning from the previous day |

When and where to seek more specialist help

09.30–10.30	Small group exercise to identify:

     — the circumstances where it would be appropriate to seek more specialist help and
     — local sources where such help can be found.
Followed by plenary review (coupled with tutor input as appropriate)

10.30–10.45   Morning coffee

Dealing with difficulties

10.45–12.30   Small group exercise followed by plenary review (coupled with tutor input as appropriate) in order to:
     — identify the types of difficulties which may arise (both in terms of victims and their recovery and/or difficulties relating to the parent organization)
     — develop realistic strategies for dealing with difficulties

12.30–13.30   Lunch

Supervision, follow-up and support arrangements

13.30–14.45   Various exercises followed by plenary discussion focusing on follow-up, supervision and support for participants

14.45–15.45   Outstanding issues, review of learning and close

Appendix 3

Further reading

Rather than offering a perplexing list of different texts, I have selected just a few which could usefully act as 'starters' for anyone from a non-counselling audience.

HELPING AND SUPPORT SKILLS

Most good bookshops will stock a vast range of excellent books on counselling and helping skills. However, the two included here are 'classics' that have been revised and reprinted many times:

- *The Skilled Helper: A Problem Management Approach to Helping*, written by Gerard Egan and published by Books/Cole—now in its fifth edition, 1993.
- *Practical Counselling and Helping Skills: How to Use the Lifeskills Helping Model*, written by Richard Nelson-Jones and published by Cassell—now in its third edition, 1993 (ISBN 0-304-32543-0).

USEFUL BACKGROUND INFORMATION

Although not directly connected with violence and crime, the following two titles will offer an insight into dealing with crisis and other forms of trauma:

- *Working with Disaster: Social Welfare Interventions During and After Tragedy*, edited by Tim Newburn and published by

Longman, 1993 (ISBN 0-582-10247-2).
- *Coping with Crises*, written by Glenys Parry and published by The British Psychological Society and Routledge Ltd, 1990 (ISBN 0-901-71582-4).

CRIMINAL AND VIOLENT INCIDENTS AT WORK

There are very few other books specifically about violence and crime at work. Of the few sources of information that are available the following would prove a useful starting point:

- The Health and Safety Executive pamphlets, 'Violence to staff': Guidance Notes for the Financial Sector (1993) and Guidance Notes for the Retail Sector (currently in preparation).
- *Working Alone: Surviving and Thriving*, written by Mike Woods and Jackie Whitehead in association with Diana Lamplugh and published by Pitman, 1993 (ISBN 0-273-60196-2). This recently published book deals specifically with the problems faced by the lone worker.

Appendix 4

Supervision and support for staff supporters

Any staff who are involved with victims on a more formal basis will require ongoing supervision and support as a matter of course. Furthermore, sooner or later they are bound to come across cases where the victims involved are more seriously affected or, where for one reason or another, the supporter becomes personally affected. In other helping or support settings ongoing supervision would be automatic. It is recognized as essential that people who provide support to others (sometimes in quite distressing circumstances) receive support themselves. They need a private, confidential forum where they can unload any personal worry or anxiety and, at the same time, receive appropriate professional guidance and help. However, unless a company employs a counselling professional, this is probably the one area where external help will be required. It is important, therefore, to spend some time looking at:

- What kind of help may be needed
- Where appropriate help can be found
- Practical ways for providing help in an organizational context

The text that follows will look at each of these points in turn.

WHAT KIND OF HELP MAY BE NEEDED?

Assuming most of the direct support work with victims is carried out by suitably trained internal staff, then typically the role of the professional supervisor will be twofold:

1. To facilitate confidential periodic supervision, review and support meetings with staff supporters. This could be carried out on either an individual or group basis depending on circumstances (though usually group meetings offer the greatest opportunity for learning for everyone who is involved).
2. To provide confidential specialist guidance with individual cases (as needed) and, where necessary, to act as a point of referral for more serious or complicated cases.

Defining these two parameters has direct implications for the skills, abilities and presence which a competent supervisor should be able to demonstrate. As a general rule these should include:

- Specific experience of working with victims of violence, crime and other forms of trauma.
- General experience of counselling across a wide range of different issues.
- An ability to recognize and work with the constraints and limitations of the particular organizational setting (I believe this is particularly important in commercial organizations which struggle to balance (and sometimes juggle) the commercial needs of the business with the needs of victims).
- However, following from the previous point, also an ability to confront and challenge the organization where policies, procedures or practice are in obvious need of reform.
- A skill (and willingness) in providing feedback which is organizationally relevant but at the same time does not compromise confidentiality with either individual supporters or victims.
- A personal 'presence' which is credible organizationally.

WHERE TO LOOK FOR APPROPRIATE HELP

Over the last decade general provisions for counselling and support have become more widely available. However, the type of supervisory help which is under discussion here is a little more specialized. Organizations that may be able to help or offer advice include:

- Victim Support
- The British Association for Counselling
- The British Psychological Society (in particular the Counselling Psychology Division)

(Addresses for all of these organizations are given in Appendix 1.)

PRACTICAL WAYS FOR PROVIDING HELP

In companies that do not have an internal counselling resource, setting up satisfactory arrangements for periodic supervisory support usually involves entering into some form of contractual arrangement with an external counsellor or counselling agency. From the company's point of view there are usually several concerns that need to be taken into account. These include:

- The need to retain some measure of control over the level of expenditure involved
- Some mechanism for obtaining feedback on the effectiveness of any provision
- The level of access or use made of any sensitive (or confidential) organizational information
- Defining the boundaries for the extent and scale of supervisory involvement (or direct involvement with individual cases)

Contrasted against this, any reputable counsellor or counselling agency is likely to have a number of other concerns, e.g.:

- Ensuring a satisfactory level of professional service for both

supporters and victims
- The degree of confidentiality that is required to operate successfully (often dictated by a professional code of conduct)
- The boundaries of the service to be provided
- Identifying an influential point of contact for dialogue and decisions about exceptional activities or events

If external supervision and support arrangements are to prove satisfactory then all of these points will require negotiation and agreement before any work is carried out. Indeed, this point cannot be emphasized too strongly, both parties must engage in open discussion of each other's expectations and come to some agreement over any points of difficulty before any work is carried out with either staff supporters/counsellors or victims. Failure to do so risks disappointment all round.

Appendix 5

Statistics on crime

The following table illustrates the trend of a few other categories
of crime that may have some relevance for incidents at work:

Offence	1989	1990	1991	1992
Total for violence against persons	176 962	184 665	190 339	201 800
Robbery	33 163	36 195	45 323	52 900
Kidnapping	516	545	766	not listed
Burglary	825 930	1 006 813	1 219 464	1 355 300
Arson	23 715	26 469	30 090	33 700
Theft and handling stolen goods	2.013 m	2.374 m	2.761 m	2.851 m

Interestingly one of the few categories of crime that has fallen over this
period is:

Theft by an employee	19 849	19 417	17 264	not listed

Source: Criminal Statistics for England and Wales, HMSO, 1992.[22]

References

1. Burrows, J. and M. Speed, *Retail Crime Costs: 1992/93 Survey*, British Retail Consortium, 1994.
2. *Violence to Staff Handbook*, Family Services Units, 1989.
3. 'Violence to staff', Report to the DHSS Advisory Committee, 1988.
4. 'Violence to staff', Health and Safety Executive Pamphlet, 1988.
5. 'Violence to staff', Health and Safety Executive Pamphlet, 1988.
6. *Yorkshire Evening Post*, 24 June 1993.
7. *Criminal Statistics for England and Wales*, HMSO, 1991.
8. Private correspondence with the Building Societies Association, 7 October 1993.
9. 'The hidden cost', a survey of bank and building society robberies commissioned by the Banking Insurance and Finance Union, 1992.
10. Beck, A. and A. Willis, 'Trouble in store', *Police Review*, 11 January 1991.
11. *The 1988 Crime Survey*, HMSO, 1988.
12. Health and Safety at Work Act, 1974.
13. Private conversation with the Association of British Insurers, October 1993.
14. Hill, C., 'Protecting employees from attack', *Personnel Management*, February 1988.
15. Hibbard, M. and J. Shapland, *Violent Crime in Small Shops*, London Police Foundation, 1993.
16. Viney, A. 'Crime in small shops', *Victim Support Magazine*, No. 52, Winter 1993.
17. Dyregrov, A., 'Caring for helpers in disaster situations: psychological debriefing', *Disaster Management*, Vol. 2, No. 1, 1989.
18. Jones, J.A.G., 'Training intervention strategies', *Training and*

Development, 1985.

19. Richards, D.A., 'Traumatic stress at work: a public health model', *British Journal of Guidance and Counselling,* 22, 51–64, 1994.

20. Horowitz, M.J., N. Wilner and W. Alvarez, 'Impact of events scale: a measure of subjective stress', *Psychosomatic Medicine,* 41, 209–218, 1979.

21. Goldberg, D. and P. Williams, *A Users Guide to the General Health Questionnaire,* NFER-Nelson, Windsor, 1988.

22. *Criminal Statistics for England and Wales,* HMSO, 1992.

Index